AF446817

# ANIMALS OF
# THE ANTARCTIC

*In the same series*
VANISHING WILDLIFE OF EAST AFRICA
Jean Bothwell
ANIMALS OF THE HIGH ANDES
Alida Malkus
ANIMALS OF THE VALLEY OF THE AMAZON
Cecile Hulse Matschat
ANIMALS OF THE FAR NORTH
Charles Paul May
ANIMALS OF CENTRAL ASIA
Edward Osmond
ANIMALS OF AUSTRALIA
Maurice Burton

# ANIMALS OF THE ANTARCTIC

Robert Burton
Illustrated by David Parry

**ABELARD-SCHUMAN**
London · New York · Toronto

J 591.999
B97

SHAKER HEIGHTS PUBLIC LIBRARY

© Robert Burton 1970
Illustrations © Abelard-Schuman Ltd., 1970

Standard Book Number 200.71653.0
L.C.C.C. No. 76-110578

All rights reserved. No part of this publication may
be reproduced, stored in a retrieval system, or trans-
mitted in any form or by any means, electronic, mechanical,
photocopying, recording or otherwise, without the written
permission of the Publisher.

| LONDON | NEW YORK | TORONTO |
| --- | --- | --- |
| Abelard-Schuman | Abelard-Schuman | Abelard-Schuman |
| Limited | Limited | Canada Limited |
| 8 King Street | 257 Park Avenue South | Scarborough |
| W.C.2 | New York 10010 | Ontario |

# Contents

70 12297 W

Antarctic scene

# CHAPTER ONE

# What is the Antarctic?

Three hundred years ago when men first began to explore the distant parts of the world, they believed there was a continent which they called Terra Australis Incognita—the unknown southern land. Expeditions went in search of this land but its discovery came gradually. It was many thousands of miles from the explorers' home ports in Europe and North America and the unknown land was guarded by fierce storms and heavy ice floes.

In 1772 Captain Cook sailed down into the southern seas but the ice prevented him from reaching land. Then some sixty years later the American Charles Wilkes, the Frenchman Dumont d'Urville and the Englishman James Ross sighted land south of Australia and the existence of the sixth continent, Antarctica, was made known.

Again there was a gap of many years until Antarctic exploration began in earnest. It was not until the beginning of the twentieth century that the first expeditions were sent down to build bases to house men on the unfamiliar land. These bases enabled the men to spend a year or more carrying out scientific observations and journeys of exploration. Some expeditions ended in tragedy like Scott's, others in failure like Shackleton's, but they formed a basis for the permanent scientific research stations that are now being operated in the Antarctic by several nations.

What is it that makes this continent so important to the men who risked their lives to explore it? First, Antarctica is one and a half times the size of Europe or the United States of America, so it was a challenge to find out what was there. Then, as more became known about the continent, it was found that in it lay information essential to the understanding of the nature of the whole world. Before we look into the details of the explorers' work we must understand broadly the main characteristics of the Antarctic continent.

On most maps Antarctica appears as one large mass of ice. This picture is oversimplified. There is land under the ice, as indeed there must be if the Antarctic is to be classed as a continent. Recent expeditions to the Antarctic, equipped with special instruments, have been able to show that the continent consists of a large land mass with islands bordering it. Some of the islands are buried in the ice sheet which is, on average, around 6,000 feet, or over one mile, thick. If all this ice were to melt at once, the oceans of the world would rise by 200 feet, completely covering most of the world's major cities.

The Arctic, too, is ice-bound, but there is nothing to compare with the thick Antarctic ice sheet. The reason for the difference between these two polar regions is that, although they are both cold because they are the parts of the earth farthest from the sun, the Antarctic is a land mass and the cold is trapped in the form of the ice sheet. The Arctic, on the other hand, is a sea, surrounded by the continents of America, Europe and Asia. The Arctic sea is frozen but ice never accumulates to the same sort of depth as in the Antarctic because the cold water and ice can flow away to the North Atlantic and North Pacific Oceans. Because the ice does not accumulate, the Arctic warms up in summer. The Antarctic has no real summer. Even on the outer edges of the continent the temperature rarely rises above freezing point, and this is only sufficient to thaw some of the snow. Where the land protrudes through the ice sheet bare rock becomes exposed and ponds and lakes may be formed.

The weather in the southern hemisphere is very much affected by the cold air that blows up from the Antarctic. The continent is saucer-shaped and as the air over it cools down it sinks into the saucer. Eventually, the air spills over the sides and spreads out, mixing with and cooling the warmer air to the north.

Not only the air but also the ice moves continually out from the middle of the continent, but of course much more slowly than the air, perhaps fifty yards a year. When it reaches the coast, the ice continues to move out over the sea but remains attached to the land, forming an "ice shelf." Occasionally pieces of ice shelf break off and float away as icebergs. It is not unusual to see icebergs 200 feet high but there will be much more ice, perhaps another 600 feet, below the surface, since ice floats very low in the water. Icebergs are often many miles in length and breadth. The largest on record would have covered an area as large as Greater London. In fact, it has been known for ships' crews to mistake icebergs for land when in thick fog.

The flow of cold air and ice cools the surrounding seas.

The ordinary maps in our atlases often show the Atlantic, Indian and Pacific Oceans as extending down to the coasts of Antarctica. However, the seas surrounding this continent are sufficiently different in temperature and salt concentration to be called the Southern or Antarctic Ocean by the oceanographers studying them. The boundary between the Southern Ocean and the other oceans runs just to the south of Australia, Africa and South America.

Like the cold air masses influencing the weather of the Southern Hemisphere, the water of the Southern Ocean influences the conditions of the neighbouring oceans. To see why, we shall have to examine briefly the flow of water currents around the Antarctic.

As sea water cools, it becomes heavier and sinks. The water that washes the Antarctic ice sheet is cold, so it sinks under the warmer and lighter water to the north. This is called the Antarctic Bottom Current, shown in the diagram (p.13) which runs along the ocean bed right into the northern hemisphere. Water that flows away from the Antarctic in this current is replaced by the Atlantic Deep Current from the tropical waters to the north. Nearer the surface there is a similar sinking of cold water under the warmer surface water to form the Antarctic Intermediate Current. This meeting of the cold and the warm surface water is called the Antarctic Convergence. It is shown on the map as a line running around the continent, several hundred miles offshore.

The currents are very important if we are to understand the habits and lives of animals living in the Antarctic, for these currents are the reason why such a cold and barren place can support the colonies of thousands of penguins, schools of whales and vast flocks of seabirds that we shall meet in later chapters.

If you were to travel from Australia or South America to Antarctica you would cross the Antarctic Convergence, and what is more, you could easily tell that you had crossed it. South of the Convergence you would immediately feel colder; a thermometer trailed behind the ship would show a sharp drop in the temperature of the sea. You would also be surprised by the large numbers of seabirds—albatrosses, cape pigeons and storm petrels, to mention a few. How is it, then, that these birds can live in such large numbers in such a cold place, when in our own much warmer country the birds have a hard time in winter as there is little food for them? If a fine mesh net was trailed alongside the thermometer you would find that, as the temperature dropped on crossing the Antarctic Convergence, you would catch an increasingly large number of minute plants and small sea creatures. Together these are called plankton, a name given to organisms, plant or animal, that float in the sea. Although some of them can swim, they are carried around by the currents.

In the tropics, where the water is warm and there is plenty of sun, the minute plants that live in the surface of the sea flourish. When they die they sink down into the Atlantic Deep Current which, as we saw earlier, is flowing toward the Antarctic. Here their bodies decompose and chemicals such as nitrates and phosphates are released and eventually come up into the surface layers. These are used for growth by the plants in the Southern Ocean which can thrive in vast numbers because the chemicals, and oxygen which the plankton need to breathe, exist in high concentrations in the cold water. In the next chapter we shall see that the minute plants are eaten by small animals, such as the shrimplike krill. These in turn are eaten by the fish, penguins, seals, whales and seabirds.

Now we can begin to see why scientists are eager to go down to the Antarctic. It is not just a frozen waste where nothing moves. The ice sheet over the continent is continually moving and changing and, more important, the currents of cold air and water stream northward to affect the rest of the world. This brings glaciologists to study the ice sheet, meteorologists to study winds and oceanographers to study the currents. Moreover, biologists of all kinds come to study the plants and animals living in the Antarctic seas. Their studies are very important as the teeming life in the seas will be a useful source of food for the ever-increasing human populations of the world. At the moment the only food coming from the Antarctic is whale meat and, as we shall see later, the hunting of whales has been so badly organized that there are relatively few whales left at all. With more specific information, the scientists may be able not only to tell us how to kill whales for food while leaving enough to breed and replenish the numbers, but also how the small animals and plants can be made into food for human use, possibly by being used as fertilizers for crops.

Some of the scientists studying the Antarctic carry out their work from ships cruising around the continent,

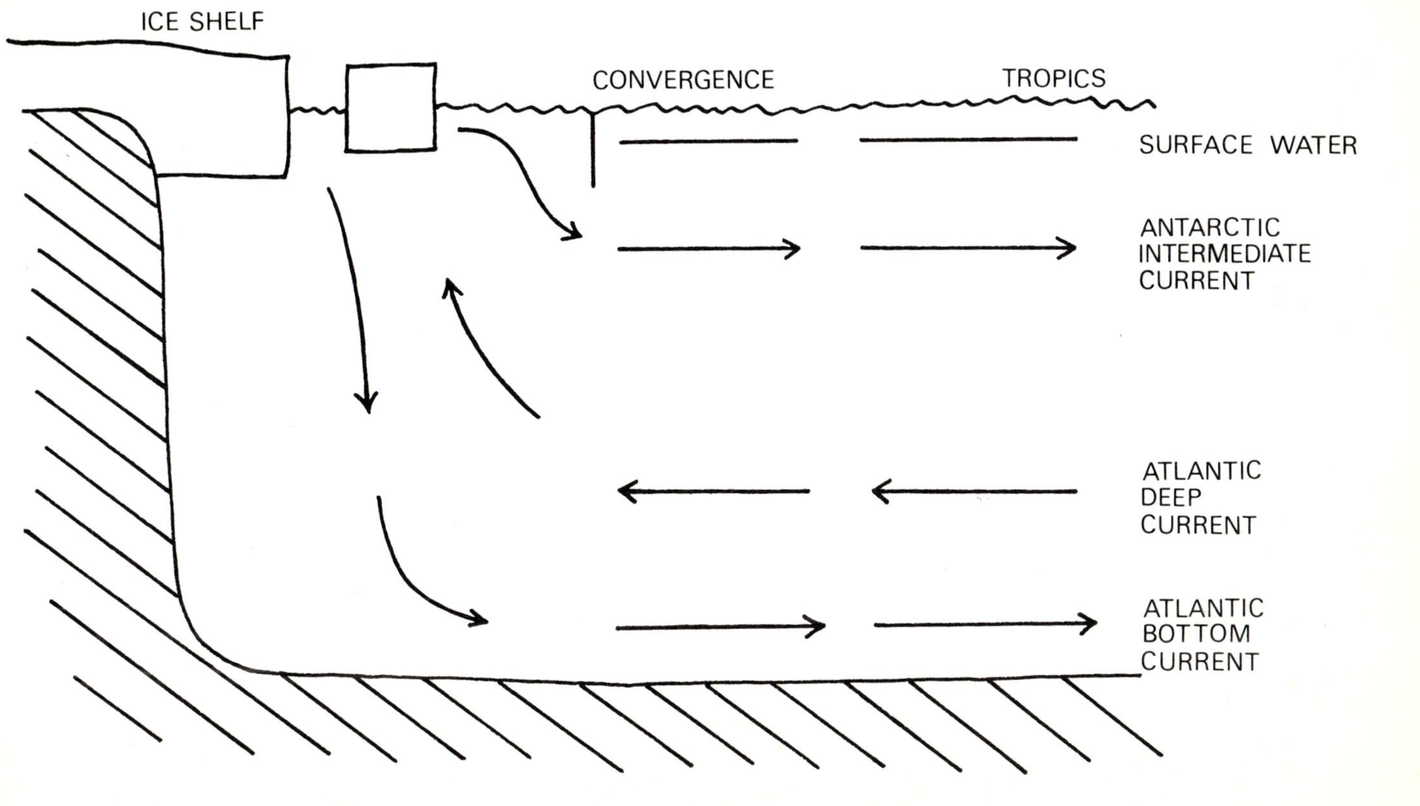

ICE SHELF
CONVERGENCE
TROPICS
SURFACE WATER
ANTARCTIC INTERMEDIATE CURRENT
ATLANTIC DEEP CURRENT
ATLANTIC BOTTOM CURRENT

catching sea creatures or recording temperatures of air and water, but many more scientists live in permanent research bases on the continent. Most of these are built on the coast so that supplies can be brought in easily by ship. From the bases, the scientists can travel out over the ice to record its movement and thickness, to catch marine creatures along the coasts or to study the habits of seals and penguins that live and breed by the water's edge. They bring back the information and specimens they have collected to the bases and sort through them in laboratories where they can work in comfort away from the cold, windy weather.

The early explorers found seams of coal in the sides of the mountains that protruded through the ice sheet. Coal is formed from the decayed vegetation of swamps which is then compressed by rock laid down on top of it. They also found fossils of luxuriant ferns and corals. Swamps, ferns and corals are characteristic of tropical regions, and this shows that the Antarctic has not always been frozen. One reason suggested for the change in climate is that Antarctica was once in a different place, nearer the Equator.

Some of the fossils that have been found are very like those found in South America and Africa, so that the question arises as to how they could occur in three places that are so widely separated. The theory is that these three continents were at one time joined together and that they have, over millions of years, slowly drifted apart. This is called the theory of "Continental Drift."

Since the continents separated, Antarctica has become covered in ice and the rich profusion of tropical life has become extinct. Biologists searching the coasts for signs of life have found only a few different kinds. Most of these could have got to the Antarctic by swimming, like the seals, or flying like the birds. These, anyway, really belong to the sea. There are only a few mites and insects on land and some small creatures in the freshwater pools. The small number of animals is not only due to the cold, but the isolation of the continent from the rest of the world in comparatively recent times may have prevented all but a few animals from reaching it.

The scarcity of animals in the South Polar regions has not deterred biologists from going to the Antarctic. Rather, it may have encouraged them as they are interested in finding out how it is that these few animals are able to withstand extreme conditions. Not only must they be able to survive the cold, they must be able to live with little water, because, although Antarctica can be said to be covered with water, it is frozen, so the animals cannot use it. Even the animals living in freshwater pools have to withstand drying up when the pools freeze in winter.

Antarctica is also of interest to biologists because it is one of the very few places in the world where Man has not disturbed the animals to any great extent. The fur and elephant seals and whales have been hunted, in some places nearly to extinction, but hunting is not the only way that Man upsets animal populations. Agriculture and the spread of cities destroy the animals' living space and industry spreads pollution. It is not just certain kinds of animals that suffer but whole communities, the plants, microscopic animals, worms, insects, as well as the birds and mammals.

The isolation of Antarctica has saved it from this. Man only landed there within the last hundred years and the climate has prevented a large-scale settlement. As a result, the communities of animals are largely undisturbed and it is these communities that are of particular interest to biologists. They are trying to find how the different animals affect each other, for instance how one kind uses another as food. We shall see examples of this in later chapters.

Within the last few years many more men have been going to the Antarctic and they are taking with them nuclear reactors, helicopters and other machines. This alarmed the biologists. Low-flying helicopters caused penguins to desert their nests, other machines could pollute the ground or the sea. Worse still, animals were being killed unnecessarily. So representatives of all the nations working in the Antarctic conferred together and decided that the whole continent of Antarctica should be declared a Nature Reserve. They decided that animals should not be killed without a good reason, such as for food, and areas where seals and penguins bred should be out-of-bounds for low-flying helicopters and aircraft. This decision is a very important and good one. In other continents the animals are being pushed out by Man's advance, or only protected in special reserves, but in Antarctica it is Man who is being kept in check. When we know more about the animal communities it may be possible to kill some kinds for food without drastically reducing their numbers. Until then they must be left alone.

# CHAPTER TWO

# Life in the Antarctic Seas

The early explorers had brought back sea creatures from their travels across the Southern Ocean, but in 1925 the Royal Research Ship *Discovery*, already famous as Captain Scott's ship, was sent down to make a thorough survey of the ocean and its inhabitants. Later, *Discovery* was replaced by *Discovery II* which continued to cruise around the Southern Ocean each year until just before the Second World War. On these voyages a vast amount of information was collected by the scientists. The oceanographers collected water samples, measuring the amount of salt in each, and the biologists collected small animals and plants from various depths of the ocean, identified them, and counted and preserved them.

Each year *Discovery* sailed along a planned course around the ocean. At intervals she would stop and the scientists, aided by the seamen, lowered nets, collecting bottles and dredges into the sea. These were specially designed to collect samples of water or plankton from a required depth. The bottles and nets, for instance, were designed to be opened and closed at pre-arranged depths, so that the sample from that depth could not become mixed with water above it while the container was being raised or lowered. Collecting samples was a tedious and often unpleasant task since it might take several hours to lower, then raise, a bottle or net. The men working the winches and hauling on ropes would get soaked to the skin as the ship lurched around in heavy seas. When a sample was hauled in, the scientists would have the unpleasant task of picking through the ice-cold mud in a dredge or sorting out animals in a tub of freezing water.

So much information was collected from these voyages that it has taken years for biologists to identify all the animals and plants brought back and to understand the importance of the information. By 1966, thirty-four large volumes had been published. Some described the habits of particular living things: how they lived, what food they ate and how they reproduced. Others showed where the organisms lived and why they lived there. By collecting animals from all over the Southern Ocean the biologists showed that one kind of animal was more common in a certain part of the ocean than in another. Often the place where an animal was common could be shown to coincide with an area of a certain sea temperature or saltiness. In fact, because samples were collected from all over the ocean it was possible to draw maps of the distribution of animals, in the same way as meteorologists draw the familiar weather maps from information they have collected about air temperatures, winds and clouds.

The vast amount of information collected by the scientists working on *Discovery* is not just of interest to other scientists. The voyages were made with the intention of helping the whaling industry (see Chapter 12).

Collecting microscopic
sea life from Discovery II

The findings of the *Discovery* voyages show the richness of the Antarctic sea life. The basis of this is the abundance of minute plants, which, as we saw in the last chapter, are very plentiful because of the nitrate and phosphate salts brought from the tropics by the currents. These plants form the food of small animals, both of which make up the plankton.

Some of the planktonic animals are quite well-known. Large numbers of them are crustaceans, the group of animals to which lobsters, crabs and prawns belong. Although there are no lobsters or crabs in the Southern Ocean, there are many kinds of prawn-like crustaceans. Most of them have no common names and are familiar only to scientists. One kind, however, does have a common name. This is the crustacean called "krill" by the Norwegian whalers. It is very much like a prawn in shape and about two inches long. Its scientific name is *Euphausia superba. Euphausia* comes from the Greek for "shining light." Along each side of the body is a row of special organs which light up at night, like a glow worm. Krill are very common animals, so imagine seeing thousands of them swimming just under the surface of the sea, each one with two rows of lights like the portholes of a ship. No wonder they are called *"superba."*

Krill was the subject of much work by the *Discovery's* biologists, not because of its pretty lights but because it is the main food of the whales that are caught in the Southern Ocean. It is also the main item of food for many of the birds and seals. The biologists counted the krill that were brought up in each net and recorded the numbers by plotting them on a map of the Southern Ocean. This showed that more krill were to be found in some parts of the sea than in others, and what is more important, where krill was abundant, the most whales were to be found. Here was a direct link between an animal and its food. The biologists also showed how the krill drifted around in the currents, and so provided a method of forecasting the whale catch. If a whaler trailed a net behind his boat and caught a large number of krill, he could be pretty certain of finding whales nearby.

Although krill are the most abundant and most important animals in the Antarctic plankton, there are many others. Very much like krill, and also forming the food of whales as well as other animals, are the amphipods. These small creatures, measuring anything from a quarter to one inch in length, belong to the same group of animals as the sandhoppers that you can find on the beach. Other animals in the plankton such as jellyfish are also familiar, but there are many more that are not well-known. Some are strangely-shaped, others are beautiful, but all have one characteristic in common: they drift around in the ocean currents. Most planktonic animals can swim to a certain extent and some have a definite vertical migration, swimming up to the surface of the sea at night and sinking during the day. Some of the crustaceans may swim up to the surface from depths of nearly 200 yards. The reason for this migration is that strong daylight is harmful to the animals so that they sink down into darker layers of the sea during the day and come up at night to feed on the tiny plants which need the surface light in order to grow.

There are other animals living at the surface of the Southern Ocean. Looking down into the inky-blue water on a calm, sunny day, you can see very pale-blue marrow-shaped creatures just over an inch long. These are the sea gooseberries or comb jellies, well-named because they appear to be made of transparent jelly with rows of combs along the body. With these combs the creatures paddle themselves along. The comb jellies are not counted as plankton as they do more than just float. They swim around actively, spinning through the water, their combs flashing gold as they catch the sun. Comb jellies are flesh eaters, catching the floating animals that come their way. The squids, relatives of the octopus with soft, bullet-shaped bodies, rings of tentacles around their mouths and large eyes, have, like the krill, rows of luminous organs, and also swim around catching planktonic animals. Squids are rarely caught because they can swim much faster than the nets can be towed.

More easily caught are the fish, some of which live in shoals, feeding on the plankton, like the herring or mackerel of our own seas, but some of the small fish caught in the nets are the young of fish that normally live on the sea-bed. These fish are slow-moving and clumsy-looking with large heads. Most of them belong to a group called the Nototheniidae, or Antarctic cod. They are not related to the familiar cod of the North Atlantic, the only resemblance being that Antarctic cod taste like real cod when cooked. Their main food is crustaceans, mainly the amphipods, but they will eat anything that comes their way and are easily caught on a hook baited with meat.

Another kind of bottom-living fish is the "bloodless" or "crocodile" fish. This is a strange creature with an enormous mouth, and eyes set on the top of its head. It too, normally lives on crustaceans, but it will also engulf other fish. "Bloodless" fish is not really a correct description of it as it does have blood. However, the blood does not have the red pigment, hemoglobin, that other animals have. Hemoglobin carries oxygen from the gills or lungs to the muscles, and without oxygen muscles will not work. The "bloodless" fish present a problem to the biologists: how can they get enough oxygen to their tissues when they have no hemoglobin to carry it there from their gills? The answer is not properly known yet but it seems that sufficient oxygen is carried to the muscles dissolved in the blood fluids.

Turning from the deep sea to the shores and shallow waters, we again find a large number of animals, many of which are similar to the animals to be found either living on our own beaches or thrown up on them after a storm. There are very few beaches around the Antarctic since the continent's coastline consists mainly of ice shelves or rocky cliffs which drop straight into deep water, but in places there are sandy or rocky beaches, some with rockpools exposed at low tide.

Antarctic beaches are bare compared with those around our shores. The most obvious difference is the scarcity of brown seaweeds that are found all the way down our beaches. In the Antarctic the rocks are covered with slippery mats of green and red seaweeds. It is only below the shore, in deeper water, that the brown kelps, some with long trailing fronds, are found. The lack of the larger seaweeds may be due to the low temperatures that would hinder their growth or to the lumps of ice that float onto the shore, ground there and rock to and fro in the waves, scraping the bottom.

In general, there are fewer kinds of animals in the Antarctic, no crabs, lobsters or beds of mussels, but kinds such as are present are there in large numbers. Among the boulders and in the pools there are limpets, winkles, little fish, sea anemones and different kinds of crustaceans. After a storm, starfish, sea shells and sea-cucumbers may be found thrown up from below the low tide mark.

In the autumn when the temperature drops, a film of ice forms on the shore and the slippery green weed is killed off, as will be most things that cannot move down the shore and away from the ice. The limpets, which feed on the green weed, move down into the deep water. Then, after the surface of the sea has frozen over, the film of ice on the rocks disappears and the limpets move back up the shore. They can shelter under boulders so that when the tide goes out the ice that is left behind does not crush them. Instead, the layer of ice which may be two feet thick or more protects the limpets from the extreme cold. It may seem strange that a layer of ice can act as a protection against the cold, but the temperature of the Antarctic sea never becomes colder than a few degrees below freezing, even in winter. The air temperature, however, will fall to many tens of degrees below freezing.

Biologists living in the research stations study the animals around the shores in the same way as the scientists on the *Discovery* studied the deep-sea creatures, but on a smaller scale. They use motor-dinghies and small nets to collect samples of animals from the coastal waters. In the last few years a new technique has been used—aqua-lung diving. This enables the scientists to study the habits of animals under natural conditions as well as to make better collections, for man is much better at picking limpets or starfish off the rocky sea-bed than is a dredge or net. Even in winter scientists can continue their work by diving through holes in the ice.

We have now met some of the animals living in the Southern Ocean but we have not gained any real idea of their numbers. If you look down into the water from a ship on the Antarctic Ocean it looks no different from the sea around our coasts. There is no sign of the teeming plankton, yet the plants and animals are there. They are difficult to see because they are very small and their bodies are almost transparent.

In order to judge the abundance of the plankton, consider one of the great whales. An average sized whale weighs forty tons, and 30,000 of them were once caught each year, giving a total of 1,200,000 tons of whale. For this amount to be killed each year there must be many more whales living, say ten times more, making a total of 12,000,000 tons of whale flesh. To produce a ton of flesh a whale must eat ten tons of krill, and similarly it will take 100 tons of minute plants to feed the ten tons of krill. This means 12,000,000,000 tons of minute planktonic plants are used for making up the whale population of the Antarctic. Then, we must also remember that not only whales eat krill, there are the seals, perhaps ten million of them, and uncounted millions of penguins, albatrosses and other birds. Most of these feed on krill. Others catch fish or squid, but these, again, feed on krill or other crustaceans. So everything depends on krill and krill depends on the minute plants—which exist in uncountable millions of tons. No wonder scientists have suggested that the contents of the Southern Ocean will help to feed the world.

# Penguins' Home Life

Penguins live only in the southern hemisphere and many people think of them as living only in the Antarctic. In fact only six of the seventeen different kinds of penguins live in the Antarctic. The rest live on the southerly coasts of Australia, South America and South Africa, with one, the Galapagos penguin, living on the Equator.

Penguins cannot fly but they can swim better than any other bird. They have been recorded as swimming at 25 m.p.h., so rivalling the speed of dolphins and seals. The special features of an ordinary bird's forelimbs that allow it to fly have been modified in penguins to increase their powers of swimming. The wings have lost the quill feathers and flexibility necessary for controlling flight. Instead they have become rigid flippers covered with small scalelike feathers. Unlike other flightless birds, such as the ostrich, that no longer use their wings, penguins, like the flying birds, have large breast muscles. This is because they are used for swimming. Penguins are often described as swimming overarm, but they use their flippers in the same way as other birds use them for moving through the air. In fact, they "fly" through the water, using tail and feet for steering only.

Under the skin is a thick layer of fat. No flying bird

would be able to carry such a weight, but it is of use to a diving bird, helping to streamline the body and, by acting as insulation, slowing down the loss of body heat to the cold air or water.

Of the six Antarctic penguins, the kings and emperors are much larger than the others. The four kinds of smaller penguin are the Adélie, macaroni, gentoo and chinstrap penguins. They are all around the same size, standing about eighteen inches high. Like all other penguins they are mainly black and white, but each species can be distinguished by special markings. The Adélie and chinstrap penguins are black and white only, but can be easily recognized. The Adélie has an all black head with white circles around its eyes so that it looks like a golliwog; the chinstrap, as its name suggests, has a band of black running around its white neck and, as a consequence, is also known as the ringed or bearded penguin. Gentoos have orange beaks and feet and a white patch above each eye. The macaronis are most attractive, having red beaks and tufts of long golden-orange feathers around the sides of the head, forming a crown.

Long before the coastline of Antarctica or any of the surrounding islands are sighted, penguins can be seen from the deck of a ship. Groups of a dozen or so can be seen jumping out of the water, then plunging back in, to reappear in a similar manner some yards farther on. This is the characteristic way in which penguins travel in water— by alternate leaps and dives.

At other times, they can be seen swimming slowly around with only head and neck showing. Every now and then they submerge, to reappear some time later. These penguins are feeding. Their diet consists mainly of small crustaceans such as krill, but fish and squid are also eaten.

The pattern of white belly and dark back is common among seabirds and it is thought that this makes them more difficult to see. To an enemy looking down from the air, the dark back of a seabird will merge with the dark water, and an enemy swimming below and looking up will have difficulty in seeing the white belly of the seabird against the brightness of the sky. Similarly, fish and other creatures that seabirds eat will get less warning that they are about to be attacked, and so have less chance of escaping.

Of the four species of small penguin mentioned, the Adélie is the only one that lives on the coasts of the Antarctic continent. The others live on the islands within the Antarctic convergence and on the northern tip of the Antarctic peninsula.

We know very little about the habits or movements of penguins during winter because they leave the breeding grounds where the biologists are keeping watch on them and move out to sea. We presume that they move around the open sea and along the edges of the pack ice, doing little more than feed. Certainly when they return to the breeding grounds in spring they are very fat and sleek.

The breeding season for these penguins starts in October or November (remember that the southern summer occurs when it is winter in the northern hemisphere). Groups of penguins make their way to the breeding grounds, or rookeries as they are called, on slopes or cliffs above the shore. Here they congregate in huge crowds and very soon get down to the business of breeding, for the babies must be able to fend for themselves by the end of the short Antarctic summer.

We will follow the events of the breeding season of one species, the Adélie. The habits of this species have been studied in great detail by scientists in the Antarctic, mainly because it happens to nest in the places most suitable for the building of scientific stations. As far as is known, the habits of the other three species follow the same general pattern as those of the Adélie.

Groups of a hundred or so penguins band together and proceed towards the rookeries, waddling along in a line with flippers held out like the arms of a tightrope walker to help balance themselves. If the surface of the ice is smooth the penguins can relieve the weary plodding on their short legs by flopping onto their bellies and pushing themselves along with their feet and flippers. This way of travelling is also used when a penguin is being chased. They can toboggan along in this fashion faster than a man can run.

The rookery is still snow-covered when the first of the penguins arrive, but the penguins do not wait for it to melt. It seems that they can recognize the position of the previous year's nest even though the rookery is buried in snow. Courtship starts as soon as they arrive at the rookeries. First, a male penguin will point his beak at the sky and slowly beat his flippers. At the same time he makes a braying call. This is called the ecstatic display and attracts a female penguin to his nest site. Then they both perform greeting displays, bowing and nodding their heads at each other. These displays help the penguins to get to know each other, and, in time, to recognize each other. Then they use the bowing and nodding in rather the same way as we use a handshake or kiss whenever we meet.

Within a few days all the penguins will have arrived. There may be up to a quarter of a million of them and the noise they make can be heard for miles across the icy wastes. Squabbling continually breaks out as each penguin tries to sort out its mate and locate its nest site from thousands of others. After a certain amount of jostling, the old birds return to last year's mate and nest in the middle with less confusion than the younger birds around the edges of the rookery. Here, there is greater bedlam as the younger birds have to find a mate and a vacant nest site for the first time.

When the pairs have settled down it can be seen that each penguin sitting on its future nest is exactly the same distance from each of the others. This spreads them out evenly. The reason for this becomes obvious when a penguin steps out of place. A nearby penguin will lean forward and scold it with raucous cackles or even peck at it. The one that is out of place will scold back but is forced to retire to its nest site. Now both penguins are leaning right forward, almost overbalancing, but their beaks do not quite meet. Thus, we can see that by having each nest so placed, the birds may quarrel, but there is little real fighting. The penguins merely argue over the garden fence, as it were. This is important later on when the eggs have been laid. Real fighting might cause the eggs to be cracked or kicked out of the nest.

A real fight breaks out when a penguin gets right out of place, into another's nest site. The owners of the nest attack it and the fight spills over into yet another site, whose owners also join in. So a free fight develops and the original trespasser is harried through the rookery until it staggers out into the open, a picture of dejection, to find somewhere quiet to recover. Anyone who has walked through a rookery will know how that penguin feels. Penguins fight by pecking or beating with their flippers. A rapid drumming by the stiff flippers with the force of the large breast muscles behind them is very painful on one's legs. But penguins are strongly built and the thick layer of fat helps prevent any real damage being done.

We might ask why the penguins nest so close together, as they would have fewer fights if their nests were farther apart. This question arises with other birds that nest in dense crowds. It is likely that the habit has the advantage that a crowd of animals is better able to ward off enemies than a single pair. It may also be that breeding activities are stimulated by the sight of similar conduct on the part of others in the rookery.

When the snow melts, nest building can start in earnest. The male collects pebbles which he takes one at a time to the female, who remains standing on the nest site. He drops each pebble in turn at her feet and they both bow and nod their heads in greeting. The female then picks up the pebble and places it in the ring of pebbles that is growing up around her. If last year's nest is still there, repairing does not take long. Otherwise the male must spend a long time collecting enough pebbles, one by one, to complete a new nest. He may have to climb down a cliff to collect each of them from the beach; but if a pair of penguins are foolish enough to leave their nest unattended, other birds will save themselves a long walk to the beach by stealing the pebbles for their own nests.

During the time of courtship and nest building both male and female stay ashore, fasting. Then, after she has been ashore for two or three weeks, the female lays two white eggs about three inches long. The two- or three-week fast and the laying of these eggs use up her food reserves. She loses the quarter-inch layer of fat that accounted for one third of her weight, so after laying she leaves the rookery and goes out to sea to feed and replenish her lost weight. The male is in a better state as he started off heavier and did not have to produce two large eggs. He stays behind brooding the eggs. Both he and his mate will have lost the feathers from a patch on their bellies, leaving an area of skin that is full of small blood vessels. This is called the brood patch and it acts as a hotwater bottle, keeping the eggs warm by the heat from the blood.

Penguins have to guard their eggs carefully. Not only must they be prevented from getting cold, but there is a danger of their being taken by enemies. Sheathbills, the small, white birds described in a later chapter, scurry through the rookeries looking for anything left unguarded.

Skuas, the brown, gull-like birds also described later are the other danger. They circle over the rookery waiting for eggs to be left unguarded, while the brooding penguins lunge up at them with their beaks. Suddenly, one will drop down into the mass of penguins, pick up an egg before it can be attacked and fly off to consume it at leisure.

Most eggs are lost from the nests of the inexperienced penguins on the edge of the rookery. These penguins are slow in settling down to brooding and, in their bickering, eggs are often kicked out of the nest. Such eggs are easy meat for the sheathbills and skuas.

However, few eggs are lost by the experienced breeders in the middle of the rookery. They sit tightly on their eggs and, being crowded together, they present a wall of beaks that the egg stealers cannot penetrate. This shows the advantage of nesting close together.

The male penguins brood the eggs for two weeks. Then the females return from feeding, having regained all the fat they lost, and take over brooding the eggs, while the males go off to sea. By now they have not eaten at all for about five weeks, so this trip to the feeding ground is essential. A few days before the eggs hatch the parents change guard again so that when the chicks emerge after about thirty-six days' brooding, both parents will be well fed.

For the first few days of their lives, baby penguins are brooded as closely as were the eggs. This protects them from both the cold and from enemies. As they grow larger they can no longer fit under the parent, who then stands to one side of the nest, still alert to ward off marauding skuas.

While the chicks are being brooded by one parent the other goes off to collect food for them, returning with it stored in the crop where it is partly digested. Returning to the nest with a full crop the adult opens its beak to the

*Nesting site, the Adélie penguin*

chick. The chick then pushes its head into the parent's mouth to take food that is disgorged.

When they are about a month old the chicks start to move from the nest and their parents guard them less vigilantly. The chicks tend to congregate in small groups, which combine until there are groups dotted about the rookery, each of about a hundred chicks. These groups are called crèches, from the French word for public nurseries.

At one time it was thought that the adult penguins that stood around the crèches were special guardians who looked after the chicks, like babysitters, while the other parents were away feeding. They would be strange guardians though, as they are just as likely to attack a chick that comes too close as to attack a skua or sheathbill. It is now known that these penguins are birds that lost their eggs near the beginning of the season. They went out to sea to feed and, having come back, do no more than stand around their nests.

The chicks in a crèche are protected from skuas merely by being huddled together. This is just as well since parent penguins only come to the rescue if they happen to be near at hand. In any event a skua is only strong enough to kill a weakly penguin chick. So it perches on a nearby rock waiting to swoop on a weak chick that has become separated from the crèche, or if it sees a feeble one in the crèche it will fly down and jostle it away from the others. As they only kill chicks that are already weak, the skuas are merely speeding up a certain death.

At intervals the parent penguins come back with their crops full of food. When the chicks were young the parents would walk up to them and the transfer of food would take place fairly simply. Now that the chicks are in the crèches a feeding ritual called the food chase takes place. The adult leads the chick away from the crèche. It runs a few yards then stops to let the chick, who is floundering over the rocks, catch up. Then the adult sets off again. Eventually the chick is allowed to take food from the parent. Afterwards, it has to make its own way back to the creche, running the gauntlet of the skuas.

It is very rare for an adult to feed a chick other than its own but the chicks sometimes fail to recognize their parents. It is quite a common sight to see an adult being followed by several hungry chicks.

One result of the food chase is to introduce the chicks to the outside world, for soon they will be leaving the security of the crèche. By that time their adult feathers will begin to grow out from underneath their thick coat of down. The down falls out and the chicks, who are now nearly indistinguishable from their parents both in color and size, are ready to go to sea. They make their way down to the shore and gather in groups at the water's edge getting ready to take the plunge. Eventually one dives in. The others follow like sheep.

Now there is another hazard. Leopard seals may be waiting for them. Swimming at full speed, a penguin can probably keep its distance from the seal's teeth and an adult penguin may be able to outwit the seal, but young penguins lack experience and fall an easy prey.

Gradually the rookeries empty, the adults also leaving as their chicks move away. Soon there is nothing left, except the half-eaten corpses of those that died through various misfortunes. The penguins will not be seen again until the next spring when they come streaming back across the ice, the older birds reinforced in numbers by youngsters returning instinctively to their birthplace.

# CHAPTER FOUR

# Emperor Penguins

One night in the winter of 1911 three men appeared at the headquarters of Captain Scott's expedition to the South Pole. The men were haggard, half-starved and their clothes were ragged and caked with ice. They had just come back from one of the most arduous journeys ever undertaken. Two of them, Lieutenant Bowers and Dr. Wilson were to perish with Scott on the way back from the Pole. The third was Apsley Cherry-Garrard who later described their journey as the "weirdest birds-nesting expedition that has ever been or will be." Their object had been to collect eggs of the emperor penguin.

On a previous expedition Dr. Wilson had noted that emperor penguins were brooding young chicks in the early spring. This meant that they must have laid their eggs during the winter. Wilson resolved to make a trip in the dead of winter to collect some eggs and this he was able to do on Scott's last expedition before they made the journey to the Pole. He hoped that a study of the embryos, the developing chicks within the eggs, would shed light on the evolution of birds from their reptilian ancestors.

This book is not the place to describe the incredible hardships of the journey or the extreme courage of the three explorers, but they served to highlight one of the many strange habits of the emperor penguin: that it lays its eggs in the middle of the Antarctic winter, when the sun never appears above the horizon and air temperatures are many tens of degrees below freezing.

The emperor penguin is the largest living penguin, standing three feet six inches high, although it is dwarfed by fossil penguins which must have topped five feet. Together with the king penguin, the emperor is placed in the genus *Aptenodytes*, separate from the other species of penguins.

Contrasted with the smaller penguins, the emperor penguin presents a picture of dignified aloofness. Its gait is slow and sedate compared with the flap and scurry of the Adélie, and it stands with its long, curved bill tilted up, as if disdainfully looking down its nose. This is due to the structure of the emperor penguin's head. The eyes are set low in the head and under a bony ridge, so to get a good look forward the emperor has to raise its head and peer under its bill. This pose sets off its brilliant plumage, for livening up the usual blue-black and white belly of penguins is a collar of brilliant yellow and orange.

The rookery from which Wilson collected his eggs was, at that time, the only known breeding place of the emperor penguin, and consequently the species was presumed to be rare, but since Scott's last expedition the coastlines of Antarctica have been explored more thoroughly and several rookeries are now known. In 1962, the known population was estimated as being about three hundred and fifty thousand, and up to one and a half million may eventually be found.

As with the Adélie penguin, the emperor is restricted to the coasts and adjacent seas of the Antarctic. In summer they spread into more northern waters to feed and are occasionally found as far north as the tip of South America. In the autumn they start moving south to their rookeries. Courtship and mating take place and the eggs are laid in early June, in the very middle of the Antarctic winter.

To anyone familiar with the breeding habits of the Adélie penguin, or with those of many other species of birds, the habits of the emperors show several unusual features. There is none of the squabbling that accompanies the nesting of Adélies. Indeed, there is nothing to squabble over, for the emperors do not hold territories, neither do they build nests. Each female lays one large egg which is carried on the feet and covered with a fold of skin. Inside this fold of skin is the brood patch, the area of featherless skin that keeps the eggs warm.

At first both the male and female share in incubating the egg, but after a few days the females leave the rookery, and the males are left in sole charge for the rest of the sixty-day incubation period. Balancing the eggs on their feet, the penguins shuffle around the rookery, huddling together in blizzards and during especially cold spells, each penguin resting its bill on the bird in front. For a bird to come into contact with the one next to it without any sign of aggression is most unusual, but this is the clue to the survival of the emperors during the incubation period. Before the eggs were laid, the penguins were able to move about freely and the exercise helped to keep them warm.

Now, the egg balanced on their feet hampers them and, anyway, exercise is undesirable as they must conserve energy during what is going to be their two-month fast. Instead they keep warm by huddling. As a bird on the exposed side of a group of penguins becomes cold, it forces its way into the middle where contact with its fellows helps not only to warm it but also to insulate it from the cold weather.

Two months later, in August, just as the chicks are hatching out, the females return. They are now sleek and well padded with blubber, and their crops are full of fish for the chicks. If, however, their return is delayed, the males are able to feed the chicks on a fluid secreted in the lining of their own stomachs.

The returning emperor penguins do not seek out their own chicks like the Adélies. The bond between the parents disappears completely as soon as the females leave their eggs with the males. When she returns the female does not recognize her mate but wanders from male to male until one relinquishes his chick for the female to brood and feed. Now the males are free to leave the rookery and trudge off over the sea ice to find open water where they can gorge themselves on fish and restore the layer of blubber they lost while incubating the egg.

As the chicks grow older they come out from under the adult and form crèches, where they huddle in bad weather. Now both parents can go off and collect food which is needed in large quantities for the rapidly growing chicks. The adults are helped by the break-up of the sea ice which reduces the travelling distance to and from the rookery.

Emperor penguins and chicks

By January, just after midsummer, the chicks begin to leave the rookery. They lose their coat of down, which reveals the adult plumage that has been growing underneath, and take to the sea to learn to fend for themselves.

In the summer before his egg-collecting expedition, Wilson had found a chick just shedding its down. It was then that he realized why the emperor penguins had to lay their eggs in the middle of winter. It is essential that the chicks become independent of the adults at a time when food is most abundant, as learning to fish for themselves is a crucial stage in their lives. Plankton and, consequently, the fish on which the emperors feed, is most abundant in late summer, so this is the time of year that the chicks must set out. If winter were to set in before they were capable of looking after themselves, they would perish. Now, emperor penguins are large birds and seven months pass from an egg being laid to the chick leaving the rookery. Consequently, if the chicks are to be grown up by January, the eggs must be laid by June, that is, in midwinter.

So the emperors are not behaving in such an absurd manner as it would appear. They are, in fact, well adapted to living in most difficult conditions. This is also demonstrated by other facts.

When the egg is laid neither parent appears very keen to incubate it, and it is passed backward and forward between the two parents. Any eggs that become abandoned are left lying in the snow. When the females have gone, any egg or chick that becomes separated from its parent is hastily picked up by any adult that has not got an egg of its own.

The value of eggs being accepted from the mate only at the beginning of the incubation is that by not picking up abandoned eggs, the males are saved from incubating frozen, lifeless eggs for two months, and enduring their long fast for nothing. Later, if a male drops his egg he, or another penguin, will immediately pick it up before it freezes, so ensuring the survival of the eggs.

There is also a value in the male taking the lion's share of the incubation. The rookeries are a long way from open sea, so it is uneconomical for the parents to keep walking to-and-fro to relieve each other. The female leaves first for she has to regain the energy lost as a result of producing an egg weighing one pound. Meanwhile the male is able to survive for two months without feeding because he remains relatively inactive and his lack of aggressiveness allows him to huddle close to those next to him.

In this way the emperor penguin is well fitted to living under what the early explorers had presumed to be impossible conditions. What we must remember is that conditions which are harsh to human beings brought up in temperate climates, are quite tolerable to an animal adapted to cope with them.

# CHAPTER FIVE

# King Penguins

King penguins look very like emperor penguins, with blue-black backs and white fronts with patches of yellow and orange around the neck. They differ in that the patches around the necks of king penguins are separated from the breast patches by a line of black, and the king penguins are slightly smaller birds. In contrast to the emperors, the kings live on the fringes of the Antarctic, from Tierra del Fuego and the Falkland Islands, southward to the South Sandwich Islands. Elsewhere, they are found on the sub-Antarctic islands of Macquarie, Kerguelen, Marion and Heard.

At one time king penguins were to be found on the South Shetland Islands, but a century ago they were wiped out by the sealers. These men originally came down to the Antarctic to collect the skins and blubber of the fur and elephant seals, but, as these animals became rarer, the sealers turned to the penguins. A king penguin is covered with a layer of blubber three-quarters of an inch thick, and there was no difficulty in rounding up penguins and slaughtering them as they stood in their rookeries. Their blubber was then boiled to extract the oil which was used for tanning leather. Within no time rookeries became deserted, but, luckily for the king penguin, it became uneconomic for the sealers to look for the few scattered survivors and the species has managed to survive. A few small colonies of king penguins exist in the Falkland Islands and near Cape Horn and there are now large numbers living on South Georgia and other islands.

When it comes to the care of the chick the king penguin has the same problem as its cousin the emperor. The chicks are very large and they grow slowly. The emperor penguin living in the depths of the Antarctic has solved the problem by starting the seven-month nursery period in midwinter so that the chick can become independent before the next winter. The king penguin has found a different solution. It lives farther north, in regions where the winters are less severe. The sea does not freeze over and the adults are always able to feed near the rookery. So, instead of breeding early, the king penguin lays her single egg in spring or summer and continues to feed the chick throughout the winter. The following spring, when food becomes more plentiful, the chick rapidly puts on weight and leaves the rookery to fend for itself. This takes place in December, that is, midsummer. It is now too late for the parents to start a new family that year, so they have a holiday, as it were, until the following spring.

This means that it takes twelve months to rear a king penguin chick, and, because the parents cannot immediately start to lay again, they can only raise two chicks every three years. This is a very slow rate of breeding, so it is not surprising that the kings quickly succumbed to the activities of the sealers.

Let us follow the habits of the king penguins in greater

detail. Just before the breeding season starts they moult. They come ashore and stand around in groups, shedding their old feathers to reveal brilliant, shiny new plumage. When moulting is complete they go back to the sea to feed and make up the weight they lost during the moult. Not only have they been standing around without feeding, but the process of making new feathers has used up a portion of their food reserves.

After a couple of weeks the penguins return. They are now in the peak of condition and ready for the job of raising a chick, a task that will take up most of their time for the next twelve months. On landing, they make their way up to the rookery. The males take up positions around the rookery and start to advertize the fact that they are in need of a mate. To do this they put on a special act or display, which is the equivalent of the songs of more familiar birds. The king penguin stretches his neck and ruffs out his feathers. Then he tilts his head until his beak is pointing at the sky, and calls. At the end of the call, which is a shortened version of his normal donkeylike bray, the beak jerks back to the horizontal and the neck relaxes. One result of his display is that nearby males peck at him, for they see him as a rival.

If a lone female catches sight of the displaying male she will wander over to him. The two introduce themselves by flagging their beaks up and down and then they set off on what is called an "advertisement walk," strutting along on their toes, swinging their heads from side to side to show off the brilliant patches of colour on their necks. It is during this walk that the two birds get to know each other.

At first the partnerships are short-lived, for the penguins go through stages of courtship, rather like humans. To begin with, the male displays at any female, and may "keep company" with a succession of females, displaying and walking with them. Gradually, however, he directs his attentions to only one female and the bond between them becomes stronger. The pair then use another display. Standing side by side, they raise their beaks into the air and stand on their toes, as if stretching themselves.

During the courtship period they select a nest site and defend it against other penguins. No real nest is made, for the king penguin, like the emperor, holds its egg on its feet and covers it with a fold of skin. However, unlike the emperor, the king penguins stay at the nest site and do not wander around with their eggs unless disturbed.

The first eggs are laid in late November and new eggs continue to appear until April. The female incubates the egg for the first few hours, then the male takes it while she goes off to feed. This is the same pattern that we saw in the emperor penguins, but now there is a difference. The female stays away for only two or three weeks as she does not have to make a long journey over the sea ice from the rookery to open water. On her return the male goes away for a similar length of time.

The eggs hatch in seven to eight weeks and for another three or four weeks the chicks stay with the parents on the nesting site. As with Adélie penguin chicks, chicks of king penguins are brooded by the parents for the first few days of their life. Then they become more independent. They come out from under the parent and stand by the nest but will dive back if danger threatens. When they get older they leave the nest sites and form crēches, while both parents leave the rookery and go fishing. The parents return each time with four to five pounds of fish and squid, and the chicks grow rapidly.

The amount of food in the sea diminishes as winter sets in. The chicks are fed less frequently, perhaps every two to four weeks, and they lose weight. But, like the male emperor penguin when he is incubating his egg, the king penguin chicks survive by keeping still and conserving energy. In the spring the adults are able to bring more food and the chicks pick up weight.

In December, a year after the eggs were laid, the best fed and largest chicks start losing their downy feathers to reveal the adult coat. Two months later they take to the sea and learn to fish for themselves. This is well-timed, because there is an abundance of food in February, just when the chicks are having to learn to fish.

Like the Adélies and other penguins, the young king penguins are liable to find leopard seals waiting for them offshore. However, the seals will find the king penguins difficult to catch for they have an efficient alarm system. If a king penguin sees a leopard, or any other seal, it panics, and strikes out wildly for the shore. In its headlong rush, the penguin thrashes over the surface of the sea, beating with its flippers. The clattering sound this makes alerts other king penguins and they all rush, clattering, to the shore. In this way, not only are all the penguins alerted, but the leopard seal is probably confused by all the flapping and beating, and will only be able to catch weak or perhaps unwary king penguins.

The young king penguins stay at sea for most of their early life. As they grow older they spend more and more time ashore and start rehearsing their displays. Then, when they are six years old, they will start courting in earnest.

In examining the breeding habits of the king penguin, we can see that they have a mixture of the habits of both the emperor penguins and the small penguins such as the Adélie. Like the emperor they build no nest, the egg is carried by the adult, and the chicks take a long time to grow up. But, unlike the emperors, the kings hold territories which they defend against intruders, and throughout the chicks' early life each is fed solely by its own parents.

These comparisons serve to strengthen the conclusions we drew in the preceding chapter that the emperor penguin is specially adapted to its unusual way of life. It has to have long spells of incubation because of the time needed for the partner to go off and feed, and it has lost its instinct to defend its nest site because of the necessity to huddle together in the cold. This is unnecessary on the sub-Antarctic islands, so their near relative, the king penguin, behaves more like other penguins.

*King penguins with large chicks changing their plumage*

# CHAPTER SIX

# The Tubenosed Birds

In Chapter I we learned that to the south of the Antarctic Convergence the seas were full of small floating animals, and that their abundance was the reason for the large numbers of sea birds that live there. A ship sailing down to the Antarctic will have been followed by different kinds of birds all the way, but as it crosses the Convergence their numbers increase and wherever one looks there are birds, large and small, flying about over the surface of the sea.

These birds are members of the Procellariiformes, more familiarly known to us at the petrels or tubenoses. The latter name describes the feature by which we can recognize them. The nostrils of most birds are merely holes in the upper half of the bill, but the nostrils of the tubenoses are placed at the end of a tube that runs along the top of the bill.

Tubenoses are ocean-living birds and are found all over the world. In the North Atlantic, bird watchers are familiar with tubenoses like the fulmars, shearwaters and storm petrels, but nowhere are there so many tubenoses as in the Southern Ocean. Here we find the albatrosses, giant petrels, snow petrels, cape pigeons, dove prions, Wilson's storm petrels and many others. Some of them range far to the north of the Southern Ocean, with the Wilson's storm petrels coming up into the North Atlantic as far as the British Isles on one side of the Atlantic and Labrador on the other. The dove prion, with its light grey plumage and matching legs and bill, breeds only to the south of the Antarctic Convergence, but it does not range as far south as the snow petrel, which is the size of a jackdaw, with pure white feathers and black legs, bill and eyes. Its range is confined to the cold waters of the Southern Ocean and together with the brown-and-white Antarctic petrel, the snow petrel is commonly found in the pack ice where they can be seen standing in groups on ice floes or fishing in the water between.

Most of the tubenoses feed on the small fish, squid and crustaceans that live in the surface layers of the sea. Flocks of them gather where the crustaceans congregate, for instance, where currents mix and form eddies or grounded icebergs rock in the swell, stirring up sand and mud from the bottom. They are frequently seen following ships because the wakes stir up the crustaceans, bringing them to surface where the birds can easily catch them.

The snow petrels paddle around in the leads, as the stretches of open water in the pack ice are called, picking up their prey one by one. The tubenoses are rather unusual because they have a well-developed sense of smell, which is rare in birds. It is very likely that they use this for finding their prey. They also have special valves in their nostrils, as do other fisheaters, like the kingfishers. When the bird puts its head underwater the valves are pushed shut protecting the delicate passages of the nose but allowing water to circulate around the sense organs.

The Wilson's petrels' method of searching for food is to fly just above the water with their legs hanging down. The wings beat just enough to keep them airborne while they literally hop over the surface of the sea. For this reason the old sailors irreverently called them "Jesus Birds," and the name "petrel" is thought to be derived from St. Peter, again because of the appearance of walking on water.

Another sailor's name for storm petrels, of which the Wilson's petrel is but one of a score of species, is "Mother Carey's chickens," Mother Carey being the English corruption of Mater Cara, a Latin name for the Virgin Mary. Despite these names the sailors considered the appearance of storm petrels around their ships as bearers of bad news, because they thought their appearance forecast the coming of stormy weather. They do indeed seem to congregate around ships in storms, perhaps because the passage of the ship leaves a patch of calmer water which enables the storm petrels to feed.

All the tubenoses have the same basic way of life which is similar to that of the penguins, to whom they are distantly related. They spend their life away from land, quartering the seas in search of food and only returning to land to breed. Usually one large egg is laid and this is brooded for fairly lengthy periods by the parents, who take turns sitting for several days each. As with the penguins the chick is brooded for the first few days of its life, then it is left while both parents go away to feed.

Tubenoses breed in colonies on cliffs and slopes overlooking the sea. There are exceptions to this, however.

A party of geologists and surveyors working in the Tottanfjella, a range of mountains at the southern end of the Weddell Sea, were surprised to see snow petrels flying around the steep rock faces of the mountains. On investigation, they found that the snow petrels were breeding and that several nests had chicks in them. It did not need an ornithologist to tell them that it was surprising to find seabirds breeding 150 miles from the sea. The birds were making a round trip of 300 miles to collect food for their chicks, an impressive feat, more especially as they would have had to contend with violent blizzards. But the interesting question is, why did they start breeding in such a remote spot in the first place? This is something we cannot answer.

Apart from the albatrosses, to be considered in the next chapter, the biggest of the tubenoses is the giant petrel, which is about the size of a goose. It is an ugly bird with a dirty grey plumage and a long, typically tubenose, beak. Sailors used to call it the Nellie, or the Stinker after its unpleasant habits. Like most of the tubenoses it will sit tight on its nest if threatened and defend itself by spitting a stream of oil at any intruder. The oil smells like strong cod-liver oil and, mixed with it, are pieces of half-digested squid and fish. The chicks are particularly good at this. When they are a few weeks old their parents leave them sitting on the nest and go out to feed. Although the chicks are unable to fly and hardly able to walk they are able to keep intruders at bay by spitting oil for at least six feet.

Although their normal food is fish and squid, the giant petrels are also scavengers and can be found hunting in

Wilson's petrel

colonies of penguins or smaller tubenoses. It is unlikely that a giant petrel could kill a healthy bird because, although good fliers, they are large, clumsy birds and are extremely awkward on the ground. Like all petrels their legs are weak and they can only waddle along on their feet with wings flapping. This ungainly gait is only sufficient to enable them to capture young or weak birds.

Giant petrels are also attracted to the carcasses of seals, where they gorge themselves with meat ripped off with their powerful bills. Thrusting their heads into the body of the seal their feathers become plastered with blood, giving another reason for calling them Stinkers. However, they often forfeit the fruits of their gluttony. With their weak legs, petrels cannot take off by leaping into the air like more familiar birds. They have to run over the ground or sea, flapping their wings to get up enough speed to become airborne. If there is a strong wind the run will be short but on a calm day take-off is difficult, and with a crop full of seal meat it may be impossible. The Stinker has to stop running, vomit up some of its food, then try again. Even when airborne it may still lose its food, for the piratical skuas may be waiting for an opportunity for an easy meal. They dive down on the giant petrel, harassing it until it jettisons its food to be able to fly away. Once this is done, the skua loses interest in the petrel and dives down to catch its spoils.

Although such unlovable characters, giant petrels have proved to be of interest to ornithologists. They nest in colonies along the tops of cliffs, where they can easily take off by running to the edge and jumping off. Their nests are made of pebbles and look very much like Adélie penguin nests. Only one egg is laid and this is incubated for eight to nine weeks before a fluffy grey or white chick hatches out. Because the chicks are sitting in the open and are unable to run away it is very easy to catch them and put numbered metal rings on their legs. Later, when they are three months old, the chicks leave the nest and fly away from the colony.

The results of ringing giant petrel chicks are spectacular. Giant petrels have been picked up all around the southern hemisphere. After leaving their nests they fly out to sea and feed. Then they appear on the coasts of South America, South Africa, Australia and New Zealand. Giant petrels are good gliders and the prevailing west wind speeds them around the Southern Ocean in a matter of weeks. Unfortunately they are unable to fly into strong winds and many of them perish as gales blow them onto the shores, where the bodies are found with rings still on their legs.

The smaller tubenoses nest in holes in hillsides or on ledges of cliffs. They are more protected against would-be enemies than the giant petrels, but many of them are still very good at spitting oil. However, they face another hazard in their tunnels or hollows. A snowstorm may cover up the entrance. Finding where the entrance is poses little difficulty, for the birds are used to coming home at night, when an overcast sky makes the hole impossible to see. How they find their nests is not known for certain. They may be able to smell the nest as they have a good sense of smell. They may also be guided by the calls of their mates who are already on the nest.

The difficulty starts once the nest is found. The birds will have to dig down through the snow. The starling-sized Wilson's petrels have been seen digging through eight or more inches of snow, but this is only possible if the snow is soft.

The chicks are also endangered if snow is blown into the hole, or if it melts, then freezes into ice. Unless this happens they will probably be quite safe as the temperature inside the burrow is fairly constant, staying above freezing point when the air outside is several degrees below freezing. What is more, a layer of snow over the entrance will help keep the burrow warm. If the parents are prevented from getting in, the chicks are able to survive for several days without food by living on their fat reserve. This is rather unusual, because, except for birds like penguins that are normally fed only at long intervals, young birds usually die if they are not fed frequently.

Wilson's petrels and dove prions are most active at their nest at night. At dusk they start flying in from the sea and, after flying around the cliffs, they settle outside their burrows. Inside the holes the incubating birds chatter and coo, calling their mates outside to come in and relieve them on the nest.

Although these smaller birds can take off without the long run that the giant petrels need, they still walk with difficulty and it is while they are sitting outside the nest that the tubenoses are likely to fall a prey to the skuas. There are usually some skua nests near the tubenose colonies and the bodies of dove prions, snow petrels and Wilson's petrels can be found strewn around them.

On a clear night skuas can be seen standing just above the entrances to the burrows. As an unsuspecting tubenose emerges, the skua pounces on it. Sometimes the skuas go further and search around the rocks, sticking their heads down into holes and clefts to see if any tubenose has built its nest too near the entrance. Some dove prions nest in tunnels dug in the moss covered banks of peat that are found on the islands around the Antarctic continent. If small prions can dig through the peat, there is nothing to stop the powerful skuas from following them, and a large hole with a pile of light grey feathers nearby often tells of a prion's fate.

Cape pigeons nest on open ledges of cliffs, but despite this they seem to be immune to the attentions of skuas. This is probably because they can fly straight on and off the nest, without having to shuffle over the ground. The skuas would have difficulty landing on the narrow ledges, but the cape pigeons can deter them by half-spreading their wings and tails and spitting oil in the manner of the giant petrels.

Apart from the skuas, tubenoses have few natural enemies. As they obtain their food from the sea, islands and barren coasts are the obvious places for them to breed. Such places are usually free from ground-living enemies, such as foxes or cats, which enable the tubenoses, as well as penguins and other seabirds, to nest in packed colonies. It is only where Man has thoughtlessly introduced rats, cats or dogs, who can ravage a colony of breeding birds, that tubenoses are threatened with extinction.

# CHAPTER SEVEN

# Lords of the Ocean

Albatrosses are among the many tubenosed birds to be seen flying about the southern seas. They are the largest members of the family, the wandering albatross having a wing span of at least eleven and a half feet. Nine of the thirteen species of albatross are confined to the southern hemisphere, breeding on islands and lonely coasts. The other four are found in the North Pacific. Although fossil remains of albatrosses have been found in England none now breeds in the North Atlantic but a few have been seen in modern times, wandering as far north as the Arctic Ocean. One black-browed albatross appeared in a gannet colony in the Faroes in 1860, and for thirty years, until it was shot, it accompanied the gannets on their yearly migrations.

The doldrums, the windless belt around the Equator, keep the albatrosses out of the North Atlantic, as albatrosses need a sustained wind for flight. They are heavy birds with small wing muscles but they can stay in the air for long periods and can cover vast distances because they can glide continuously over the surface of the ocean on their large wings.

The seas south of the continents of Australia, Africa and America are the true home of the albatrosses. Here the winds sweep around the world unchecked by any land mass and the albatrosses glide around with the wind, coming to land only to breed. Every ship sailing through these seas is followed by an escort of albatrosses, continuously gliding around the ship on their immense wings or hovering effortlessly above the decks. The wandering albatross is one of the commonest of the Antarctic albatrosses; others frequently seen flying around ships include the black-browed, light-mantled sooty and grey-headed albatrosses.

A wonderful view of the hovering albatross can be had from the bridge of the ship. Binoculars are unnecessary for examining this large bird at such close quarters, as it hangs poised motionless and apparently almost lifeless, for its eyes neither move nor blink. Yet the bird is alert to the slightest change in the wind, allowing for it by delicate movements of the wings, until it suddenly flips one wing and breaks away to circle the ship, rising and falling with a beat of the wings.

Albatrosses may stay with a ship for days before continuing their flight around the ocean. Their flight is as effortless as their hovering, for with their great wingspan they are very efficient gliders, making use of every eddy of wind to keep aloft. Sometimes their feats appear impossible, as when an albatross comes shooting along past the ship for a considerable distance, its body only a foot or two above the waves, before soaring up again. Even the best glider has to lose height to maintain its forward speed, yet here is a bird gliding perhaps two hundred yards or more without losing any height, and at a considerable speed. A more careful watch will show that the albatross is gliding parallel to the swell, keeping just above one wave. It is being held aloft by the eddy currents formed as the wind is thrown up by the wave.

This habit is not sufficient to keep an albatross in the air all the time, especially if the sea is calm. Sometimes an albatross can be seen coming past the ship without pausing to hover around. It will be alternately diving down to sea level, then turning nearly 180° and soaring up to about fifty feet, to repeat the dive.

If measurements of the wind speed are made near the sea surface and again fifty feet above it, we would find that the speed is lower near the surface. This is due to friction with the surface slowing the wind down. The albatross is using this to give it extra lift. First it dives downward, a long shallow glide with the wind sweeping it ever faster, then it suddenly swings around in a steep bank, with the wingtip sometimes cutting the water, and soars upwind. It will have gained considerable momentum from its downward rush and this provides the energy for the soar, but not sufficient to bring it up to the original height of fifty feet. The little extra lift needed is provided by the increasing wind speed the albatross meets as it gains height. The albatross loses speed relative to the sea beneath it as it travels upwind, but because it is rising into ever increasing windspeeds, its speed relative to the wind, the airspeed, is not dropping so rapidly. In other words, the speed at which the air flows over the wings, which determines the lifting force, is not dropping as fast as it would if the windspeed never varied. By the time the albatross is about fifty feet up, the wind is no longer increasing and the albatross is hanging almost motionless, whereupon it tilts over and dives down again, gaining extra speed by partly folding the wings to reduce air resistance. Provided there is sufficient wind, which need not be very strong, the albatross can continue diving and soaring for mile after mile and hour after hour, using hardly any energy. All that is needed is an occasional flap of the wings.

In sub-Antarctic latitudes where the "Roaring Forties" and the "Howling Fifties" sweep around the world there is nearly always sufficient wind to keep the albatrosses aloft, and it is a very rare day when the weather is flat calm and the albatrosses have to settle on the water. Because they are heavy birds with comparatively small wing muscles, they soon tire of flapping flight. Taking-off is also difficult because their legs are weak as well, and they cannot beat their wings too hard without hitting the water. So the only way to get off is to run across the water flapping as much as possible until a combination of running and flapping provides enough lift to become airborne. It is a ludicrous sight to see an albatross pounding laboriously across the water, neck outstretched and long wings flapping, but the moment it has taken off and the legs are tucked up it is transformed into a picture of grace and elegance.

The inexpressive, fixed facial expression of albatrosses as they hover alongside a ship is probably the cause of nicknames given to them by sailors; for instance, Mollymawk (from the Dutch "mal"—foolish and "mok"—gull) and Gooney (from an English dialect word for a simpleton). To watch their wheeling and soaring must have

*Albatross*

helped relieve the monotony of long voyages, and when merely watching them had palled, the monotony of life and diet could be reduced by catching them. Albatrosses will readily land in the wake of a ship to eat any refuse thrown overboard, and, it has been said, they will attack sailors who have fallen overboard. Knowing this, sailors use an ingenious device to catch albatrosses. They tie a piece of metal, in the shape of a hollow triangle, to a line and trail it from the stern. It flashes through the wake and an albatross, mistaking it for something edible, snaps at it. Immediately the lure is pulled away, but the hook on the albatross's beak gets caught on the triangle and, as long as the line is being pulled in, the albatross cannot get away.

In the spring the albatrosses return to the breeding grounds on the cliffs of the sub-Antarctic islands, where they nest in thousands so that from a distance the tops of the cliffs may look white with closely-packed birds. In other places they nest amongst clumps of tall tussac grass and each pair is well separated from the others. The nest itself is made of tussac grass and other vegetation bound together with mud to make a steep-sided mound with a depression in the middle where the solitary egg is laid.

Much of the breeding cycle of the wandering albatross, the best known of all the Antarctic albatrosses, reminds us of the king penguins who are often found breeding on the same islands. The similarity between the way of life of the two birds has been put forward to support the idea that albatrosses are related to penguins; one having mastered travel over the sea, and the other in it. Both quarter the sea in search of fish, squid and crustaceans, and both return to their breeding grounds in early spring.

The male albatrosses arrive at the colony before the females and take up posts by their nests. When the females arrive, each one is mobbed by a throng of males as she lands. They leave their nests and gather round her, striving for attention until she accompanies one, perhaps her mate of previous years if he is still alive, back to his nest. Courtship now starts and a weird and ungainly ballet unfolds as the two enormous birds get to know each other. They keep up a continual conversation of low-pitched braying noises, bowing low to each other at the same time. This will be kept up for a quarter of an hour, and between sessions they gently nibble each other's bill and the short feathers around their partner's face and neck. At other times they rattle their bills with a quick clapping of the upper and lower mandibles, while bubbling sounds come from far down their throats. Every now and then the braying gets louder and the male bends his neck over backward until his bill is buried in the feathers of his back.

The final phase of the courtship is spectacular both in its movements and the sheer size of the participants. The male stands up, stretches his neck to the sky and unfurls his eleven-foot span of wings, curving them round to the front. In this pose, with tail raised and fanned out, he prances around, dancing with his great webbed feet and squealing like a pig. His partner becomes caught up by his excitement, sidestepping around him, with her wings held out, so that they are always breast to breast. Then suddenly they collapse, the dance is over and mating takes place.

The large, single egg is brooded by each parent in turn for nearly three months before a white fluffy chick emerges to spend an even longer time sitting on the nest before taking to the air. For the first three or four months of its life its parents bring back food every ten days or so and the chick grows rapidly. Then the winter sets in and the amount of food the parents can find drops. So, like the nearby king penguin chicks, the young albatrosses weather the winter in the colonies, gaining weight slowly and waiting for summer before leaving the colony to set off on their own.

When the chick has flown it is too late for the parents to start breeding again, so the large albatrosses, like the wanderers, breed every other year only. Their chicks fly off round the world, gliding about in the "Roaring Forties" to return several years later, if they have survived being blown ashore by gales. For the first two or three years that the young albatrosses visit the colony they only play at courtship, never getting as far as egg-laying. Eventually, when they are about ten years old, they settle down to raise offspring, each having chosen a mate with whom they will pair each time they breed.

# CHAPTER EIGHT

# Skuas and Other Birds

Around the coasts of Antarctica and the sub-Antarctic islands, wherever there is ground free of snow in summer, colonies of the great skua can be found. This is a relative of the seagulls, a little larger than a herring gull and more heavily built. Its plumage is brown, flecked with yellow or white on the neck and reddish-brown on the back, and when its wings are spread each shows a white bar. The beak and legs are dull black, the former is armed with a hawklike hook and the latter with strong claws.

Skuas have been seen farther south than any other animal. One was seen flying around the South Pole by the Americans stationed there. Why it should have flown so far inland no one knows, but this is not the only instance of their being found inland. They have been known to follow explorers and take scraps left by the husky dogs, and skuas were seen near the snow petrel nests in the Tottanfjella.

Skuas attracted the attention of the early explorers, and they still draw the attention of any visitor, for they defend their nests very vigorously. If anyone approaches a nest, the pair of skuas owning it fly out and start attacking. They swoop down at him, then, just before they crash into him, they lower their feet, twist their wings and soar away and up to repeat the attack. When these attacks become violent, the skuas come nearer and often hit the intruder with their wings and feet. During the attacks the skuas give voice to a stream of raucous cries which tell other skuas that there is danger nearby.

The cause of this commotion are two green-brown eggs speckled with dark spots that lie inconspicuously in a nest which is little more than a depression in the ground, perhaps lined with some pieces of moss or lichen.

The eggs are incubated by both parents for a month, but unlike the penguins and tubenoses, each skua sits on the nest for only two or three hours at a time. At the end of the month light-brown, fluffy chicks emerge. Within a few hours they leave the nest and wander around but will return and climb under the parent to keep warm. As they grow older they spend more and more time away from the nest until it finally ceases to have any significance for them. Instead they lie in natural depressions in the ground or snuggle up against the sides of rocks. As they are light-brown, they are very difficult to see and an enemy is likely to overlook them if it is being attacked by the parents.

When they are not brooding or guarding the eggs or chicks the parents fly off in search of food. Their feeding habits led Robert Cushman Murphy, a famous American ornithologist, to describe skuas as "gulls that have turned into hawks." The hooked beak, strong claws and powerful flight give skuas their hawklike appearance but, first and foremost, they are gulls. Their main food is fish which are caught by the method used by gulls. They circle around above the surface of the sea and when they see a fish they drop headfirst, plunging into the sea. The wings are only half-closed as they hit the water and no more than the head and neck are submerged. This is called plunge diving. A small fish can be swallowed immediately, but larger ones have to be taken to the shore to be eaten. Even in the Antarctic summer the seawater is cold enough to freeze on the feathers and skuas can be seen coming back to their nests with a crust of ice on the head and neck.

When the parent returns to the nest area the chicks run forward, squealing, and start to peck at its beak. This is the signal for it to regurgitate food from its crop, and hold it in the tip of the beak for the chicks to peck. When the chicks are a fortnight old the food is dropped on the ground and the chicks have to pick it up for themselves.

Skuas are hawklike because they also prey on other birds. They chase the small tubenoses and hunt for their eggs and chicks, digging them out of their burrows, as has been described in Chapter 6. It is true that some of the larger species of gull also hunt for prey beside fish and other marine animals, but none do it so regularly as the skuas. Nevertheless, even though they kill so many tubenoses that the area around their nests becomes littered with their remains, the skuas still show that they are really gulls. Even with their powerful beaks they are not very good at tearing up their prey. They do not hold the food down with their feet as will a hawk, but merely fasten onto a piece of flesh and tug until it comes away. Unless a pair of skuas are co-operating, each pulling a different way, the carcass just gets dragged over the ground.

Skuas also prey on the eggs and chicks of penguins.

Every penguin rookery has its attendant pairs of skuas, as both species nest on flat, snow-free ground. In the spring the skuas stand on rocks overlooking the penguin rookery or circle a few yards above the heads of the brooding penguins, waiting for one of them to relax its guard on the eggs.

Sometimes skuas hunt in pairs and use a trick to steal eggs being closely guarded. While one skua provokes the penguin to lunge forward, the other comes up behind and snatches the egg. The stolen eggs are carried away from the penguin rookeries, a hole is pecked in the shell and the contents sipped at leisure.

The killing of penguins' chicks was another reason for the explorers' dislike of skuas. At the end of the breeding season the penguin rookeries are littered with the pathetic remains of penguin chicks. Any of the explorers who stopped to watch the penguins would probably have seen a skua despatching a chick, pecking at its head and neck until it became too weak to escape. Before its struggles ceased the skua would have started to tear at its body.

Only when ornithologists spent a long time watching penguins and skuas and counting the number of chicks killed was it found that skuas are not really as black as they are painted. They are only able to kill chicks that become separated from their parents or are already weak, so they are only weeding out the chicks that are already doomed. Unless penguins, and every species of animal for that matter, lost most of their offspring before they have grown up there would soon be so many of them they would run out of food.

Skuas

Skuas spend only a short part of the year in the Antarctic, arriving in the spring and flying away at the end of the summer to the tropical seas. Their near relative, the dominican gull, lives and stays near its nesting ground throughout the winter. This gull, which lives along coasts from South America and New Zealand down to the Antarctic peninsula, is very similar to the black-backed gulls of Europe both in plumage and way of life. It is more dependent on sea food than the skua so it has a difficult time in winter when the sea has frozen over. It has to search for its food in cracks and pools in the ice, and occasionally kill small tubenoses.

The dominican gulls like to eat limpets which they manage to collect even when the sea is frozen over, by getting down into cracks in the ice. They have been described as the best Antarctic gardeners because the ground around their nests becomes littered with limpet shells. Not all of the flesh is digested so pieces left in the shells fertilize the ground for the mosses and grass that grow in the fringes of Antarctica.

Another relative of the skua is the Antarctic tern, which also only comes to the Antarctic for the breeding season. Antarctic terns are very like the Arctic terns which breed over a large area in the northern hemisphere, from Alaska and Siberia south to the British Isles and New England. Both species have white and pale-grey bodies with black caps on their heads. The Arctic tern is interesting because although it breeds in the far north, within 600 miles of the North Pole, it migrates to Antarctica for the southern summer.

Another bird that lives on the fringes of Antarctica is the blue-eyed shag, one of the many species of long-necked shags and cormorants that live around the coasts of the world. It gets its name from the ring of bright blue skin around each eye. Shags nest in colonies on rocky ledges of cliffs. Their nests are made of mud and seaweed and are used year after year.

Shags feed on fish which they catch by diving. They do not use their wings underwater, like penguins, but swim with their webbed feet. They go out feeding in flocks, flying one behind the other a few feet above the sea. When they land on the sea, they gather in a tight group called a raft and swim around together, occasionally putting their long necks under to look for fish. When one spots a fish it dives, followed by the others. They disappear for half a minute then start popping up some distance from where they submerged. Dominican gulls and skuas are attracted to these rafts of shags. They hover just above the sea and dive in as the shags surface with their fish. Quite often they can wrest a large fish that a shag has been unable to swallow immediately.

There is one bird living in the Antarctic that is not a seabird. This is the sheathbill, a white, pigeon-sized bird distantly related to the waders. It has no webs between its toes and only goes into the water to bathe. Sheathbills nest in crevices between rocks and feed along the shore where they pick up limpets and small crustaceans. In the winter some of them fly north to South America but the rest stay around the frozen shores catching crustaceans in gaps between the ice floes and searching for scraps of anything edible. They gather to pick at the flesh of wounded seals or at the corpses of chicks in the penguin rookeries. This precarious living keeps them alive until summer when they haunt the penguin rookeries competing with the skuas for abandoned eggs and dead chicks, running nimbly between the nests avoiding the lunges of the penguins. They have also developed an unusual trick for stealing the penguins' food. They will fly at a penguin while it is feeding its chick and flap at its head. This startles the penguin so that it jerks its head away from the chick. The food it was disgorging is spilt on the ground, where the sheathbill lands and retrieves it, thus getting an easy meal.

# CHAPTER NINE

# Seals in the Ice

After the penguins, the seals are the best known and the best liked of the Antarctic wildlife. Their plump furry bodies look cuddly and their big round eyes, often running with tears, give them a most pathetic, appealing look. At closer quarters they are, perhaps, not quite so charming. Their breath smells of fish and they are endowed with sharp teeth. Nevertheless, until they are disturbed they are rarely aggressive, for Man usually meets seals only when they have come out of the water to bask. In this situation they are unwilling to be aroused. If they are awakened from their sleep they will grumble but may go back to sleep even if the source of their annoyance stays put.

By and large, seals appear to live a pleasant life, sleeping and eating the year round and only stirring into action during the breeding season. But we have little idea of what goes on in their real home underwater, although in the Antarctic, biologists are beginning to penetrate this world. As the sea is frozen, it is possible to walk out over the seal's home, then enter into it by means of aqualungs or special underwater observation chambers.

This chapter deals with the truly Antarctic seals, the leopard, crabeater, Ross and Weddell seals. These, together with the elephant seal of the next chapter, belong to the

family of true seals. True seals have no visible ear flaps or
pinnae, and their hindflippers are held backwards, so that
they are very ungainly on land. They move by jerking the
body forward, perhaps assisted by the front flippers.
Although useless on land, the hindflippers are extremely
efficient paddles in the water.

The other family is the eared seals, which include the
sea lions and fur seals. They have small external ears and
can tuck their hindflippers under their bodies and bound
along on all fours. They use their front flippers for
swimming.

The leopard seal gets its name from the spots on its
throat, shoulders and sides. Yet the name leopard also
conjures up the idea of a stealthy animal, ready to leap out
at unsuspecting and unprotected passers-by. The leopard
seal has for long been credited with such a disposition and
this is reinforced by a sinister, almost reptilian, head that
makes the seal look like an extinct dinosaur. This head is
disproportionately large for the ten or twelve-foot body
and the widely gaping mouth is set with rows of sharp
teeth. It is small wonder that such an animal figures in
stories as a maneater that comes out onto the ice to chase
and kill explorers and their dogs.

These stories, are, however, unfounded, as are most
stories of unprovoked attacks by animals. It is very likely
that in these cases it is man that made the first move by
provoking the seals, whether with the intention of killing
them or merely through the strange human habit of teasing
animals.

The leopard seal's bad reputation is probably based on

its inquisitive nature. Stories of attacks on Man probably arise from the seal's curiosity which makes it go towards a man. Perhaps it then becomes a real attack because the man, seeing a 600-pound seal bounding over the ice toward him, thinks that he is in danger and tries to defend himself. Leopard seals will also follow small boats, leaping out of the water a few yards behind the boat. Again, this gives the crew the impression of being chased. It can be quite frightening, as is the leopard seal's habit of craning its neck to peer over the gunwhale. In recent years aqualung divers have been working in the Antarctic, as part of the marine biology programs. They have reported seeing leopard seals swimming around them but they have never stayed down in the water to see whether it is only curiosity which has attracted the seals.

Despite the attention that has been paid to the leopard seal, very little is known of its habits. It is not very common and it lives a solitary life on the fringes of the pack ice. In the winter most of them migrate north and then they are found around South America and Australia.

The one place where the habits of leopard seals have been at all well studied is at the penguin rookeries. This is where biologists collect in summer to watch the penguins. They are then well-placed to watch the leopard seals which lie in wait just offshore to catch penguins as they stream to and from the rookeries.

In a straight race over a short distance penguins can usually outswim a leopard seal, and we have seen that king penguins have an alarm system that warns them of danger. So the leopard seals have to resort to stratagems, such as waiting under the edge of the ice, or they have to wear the penguins down by chasing them around.

Once the penguins have got clear of the water they are safe because leopard seals very rarely hunt on the ice floes or on land, and when they do try the penguins easily outrun them.

When it has caught a penguin the leopard seal will frequently grasp it by one part of the body and, holding its head out of the water, thrash to and fro until the penguin's skin has torn loose and turned inside out. Throughout the summer the remains of penguins can be found washed up on beaches around the rookeries. They consist of the backbone and leg bones intact with the skin attached to the feet.

At first sight this habit would suggest that leopard seals are very finicky feeders, skinning their prey before eating it, but this would be a strange trait in an animal equipped with so large a mouth and teeth. What is more likely is that the seals are merely playing with their food. They have also been seen tossing pieces of seal blubber in the same way. This sort of procedure is common among other flesh eaters, as for instance domestic cats playing with mice that they have caught.

Because leopard seals are most commonly seen near penguin rookeries, it was for a long time assumed that penguins formed the bulk of their diet, but this was because the biologists only saw them feeding at the penguin rookeries. In fact, only a few of them frequent the rookeries during the summer. The rest spend their time in the pack ice or out at sea where they feed on a wide variety of items including fish and squid, and the carcasses of whales and seals. They will even attack and devour the pups of other seals.

Although the leopard seal is well-named, both on account of its spots and its predacious habits, this cannot be said of the crabeater seal. It was given this name because it has strangely-shaped teeth, each bearing a number of points or cusps. Teeth with sharp points are characteristic of animals that live on hard-bodied animals like crabs, so it was presumed that this was what the crabeaters were feeding on. This idea had to be revised when it turned out that there are no crabs in the Southern Ocean.

Crabeater seals feed almost exclusively on krill, and the cusps on the teeth serve a very different purpose from that of crushing hard prey. The crabeaters swim through a mass of krill with their mouths open, sucking it in as they go. Then the mouth is shut so that the cusps of the teeth are interlocked. The tongue is raised, water is forced out through the closed teeth and the dry mouthful of krill is swallowed. This system of sieving food is the same as that used by the whalebone whales.

If you close your mouth then feel to the back of your mouth with your tongue, you will find that there is a gap on either side, to the rear of the last cheek tooth. Crabeater seals have a special ridge of flesh which fills this gap and prevents the krill from escaping.

Crabeaters are the most numerous of the Antarctic seals. There are perhaps 5,000,000 of them as compared with 500,000 Weddell seals. Despite their abundance we know little more about their life than we do of the leopard seals. Crabeater seals also live in the pack ice and although they often haul out onto the ice floes in large groups, they breed in solitude. This has been a blessing to the seals because in recent years expeditions have penetrated into the pack ice in early spring to hunt for pups. They found that the pups were so widely scattered that it was not worth the time and expense collecting them. The adults, which do gather in groups, are of no value to the seal hunters because their skins are spoiled by the scars of wounds inflicted either by fighting each other or by their worst enemy, the killer whale. It is not at all rare to see a crabeater seal with huge scars running down its body showing that it has managed to evade a killer whale's attack.

The third seal of the pack ice is the Ross seal. This has a very distinctive shape, a large round body with a small blunt head and small mouth. Its big, bulging eyes enable it to see well in the dim light under the pack ice.

The Ross seal is very rare and little is known about it. The British explorer Ross first found it in 1840 and the specimens he collected for the British Museum resulted in the species being named after him. Over the next century only about fifty specimens were found. This was because the Ross seal lives in the depths of the pack ice fields which ships were unable to penetrate. Unlike the other Antarctic seals it has never been found north of the Antarctic Convergence, or within sight of land. It is only since the Second World War, when many more expeditions have been going to the Antarctic and icebreakers have been able to penetrate the pack ice with ease, that the Ross seal has been found in greater numbers. It is still considered rare, with an estimated population of 20,000, so it is not surprising that little is known of its habits. It feeds mainly on squid and has sharp curving teeth that enable it to grasp their slippery bodies.

The Weddell seal is also named after a British explorer. Twenty years before Ross's expedition, James Weddell was sailing into the sea that also bears his name. On his way he landed at the South Orkney Islands where he found some seals which he called Sea Leopards. Weddell seals do indeed look like leopard seals as they also have spots on the throat and chest, but they are now known not to be related to the true leopard seals. Their heads are smaller and their bodies are tubby, eight to ten feet long and 600 pounds in weight.

The habits of the Weddell seals are different from those of the other Antarctic seals. They live closer to the shore, even coming on land to breed if the sea is not frozen. This makes them very much easier to study and biologists of several nations have been studying their habits. Numbered tags of the type that farmers clip onto the ears of cattle can be attached to the webs of the seal's hind flippers. In this way individual seals can be recognized and the biologists can plot their movements, calculate how long they live and find out at what age they start breeding.

Throughout the winter the Weddell seals live under the sea ice. They only occasionally haul themselves out through the breathing holes which they keep open by chewing the ice as it forms. More frequently, the seals merely push their snouts up through a hole when they want to breathe. They even sleep hanging vertically in the water with only the tips of their noses above the surface.

When out of the water, Weddell seals breathe more slowly than we do, and they can hold their breath for a long time while fishing or travelling from one hole to another. The record for staying submerged is held by a Weddell seal that was recorded as diving for forty three minutes. Weddell seals will also sleep underwater, floating against the underside of the ice until they need to breathe.

In the very early spring female Weddell seals come out of the holes and cracks in the ice in order to give birth to their pups. The process of birth is very rapid and must present a great hazard to the pup. At one moment it is in the warm body of its mother, the next it is lying on the surface of the ice. Its body has to adjust to a change in temperature of over 100° Fahrenheit in as many seconds. The newborn pup is little more than a bag of skin and bones with large, appealing eyes. At first it is able to do little more than flop around, heaving itself up to its mother on its flippers and bleating pathetically.

An unusual feature of true seals is that their adult teeth are already appearing when they are born. The milk teeth are grown then reabsorbed into the gums before birth. However, the young Weddell pup will not need its teeth for the six weeks that it lives on its mother's milk.

The changes in mother and pup during this six weeks are most striking. Before the pup is born the mother is so fat she has difficulty in moving over the ice. But until the pup is weaned she does not feed, so she loses weight rapidly

*Weddell seals*

while the pup avidly feeds on her very rich milk. From sixty pounds at birth the pup gains about 200 pounds in six weeks. Now it is the female who is emaciated, having lost 300 pounds of blubber to provide milk for her pup.

The reserves of fat that the pup accumulates are very important because they enable it to survive while it learns to feed itself. The pups can swim when they are only a few days old, their mothers leading them to a hole in the ice and coaxing them into the water. Once in, the pups swim immediately, but being able to swim is easy work compared to being able to catch fish. One can look down through cracks in the ice and see mother and pup swimming together in the clear water, so it is possible that the pups are taught how to fish by their mothers.

The pups also have to face the chances of being crushed by the ice as it breaks up or being eaten by leopard seals. Killer whales are not such a danger because they do not usually come into shallow water.

We do not know much about the Weddell seals after the pups and their mothers have left the breeding grounds on the ice. They can be seen swimming underwater or sleeping out on the ice or on beaches. By listening carefully, strange high-pitched trills, squeaks and grunts can be heard from under the ice. Occasionally bull seals are found with cuts all over the body and sometimes they are seen fighting each other around the ice floes. The mating season starts when the females leave their pups. How the courtship proceeds is not known for certain, but American biologists are now studying the Weddell seal by following them under the ice with aqualungs.

They have found that the Weddell seals hold territories which are linked with the breathing holes. The trilling sounds that can be heard by a man standing on the ice are warnings to intruders given by the territory owner. Other males are allowed in the territory providing they keep clear of the owner. If they fail to heed his trill warnings he will attack them, and these are the fights that are occasionally seen. Serious injury rarely results because the Weddell seal's teeth are blunted from chewing holes in the ice, and their bodies are protected by the layer of blubber. On the other hand, the contestants' flippers are often mutilated and sometimes the seals are blinded.

The Americans also attached depth gauges to the Weddell seals to see how deep they dived. When the seals surfaced again at their breathing holes they were recaptured and the instruments removed. The results of these experiments showed that the seals rarely dived to depths greater than 100 yards but occasionally they would go to 300 or 400 yards. The greatest depth they ever recorded was 650 yards, which was as deep as the seal could go in the area where the study was made, and the longest dive lasted for forty three minutes.

To be able to perform such dives the seals must be well adapted to underwater life. For one thing there must be an adequate supply of oxygen to the brain while the seal is holding its breath and it must be able to withstand great pressures on its body. One of the hazards human divers face is a painful condition called the bends. This is caused by surfacing too quickly from great depths. When the lungs are under pressure nitrogen in the air becomes dissolved in the blood and it makes its way to the tissues, especially the fatty coverings of the nerves. As the diver surfaces, the pressure is released and the nitrogen forms bubbles in the same way as the carbon dioxide does when a bottle of tonic water is opened. The bubbles disrupt the nerves causing paralysis and even death.

To avoid the bends seals breathe out just before they submerge. This reduces the amount of air left in the lungs to a minimum. Any that is still left behind is contained by valves in specially rigid parts of the lungs which will not be compressed at great depths and do not absorb the air so easily as other parts.

A seal has seventy per cent more blood in its body than a human and its muscles contain large amounts of myoglobin, a chemical similar to the hemoglobin in blood. These chemicals act as oxygen stores, but a large supply of oxygen is not enough. To stay submerged so long the seal must conserve this supply. As soon as it dives, its heart beat slows right down, from around 140 beats per minute to about ten. The blood supply to the skin and digestive system is closed down so that as much blood as possible can be sent to essential organs such as the brain. When the seal surfaces again, the heart beat speeds right up and it pants for a short time so that oxygen is rapidly taken all around the body to replace that used up in the dive.

# CHAPTER TEN

# Elephant Seals

A visitor landing on a beach at one of the islands surrounding Antarctica will be struck by an overpowering smell. He will also hear weird noises like giants belching or lions roaring, with occasional terrier-like barks. The visitor will then know that he has arrived at the home of the elephant seals. At the top of the beach, above the high tide mark, the ground will be bare of vegetation and here and there will be deep, muddy depressions. These are the elephant seals' wallows. Each wallow will be filled with the bodies of elephant seals that lie piled on top of each other. Most of them will be asleep, gently breathing like so many steam engines standing in a station. Others flop around, jostling to get into comfortable positions. This leads to bickering, and the strange noises are the grumbles of elephant seals being awakened from their sleep.

The wallows are occupied throughout the southern summer by seals that have come ashore to moult. This takes about six weeks, during which time the skin and hair shreds off in pieces to reveal the new coat underneath. Not surprisingly, this causes the seals a certain amount of discomfort. As they lie there, they can be seen vigorously scratching their bodies with the claws of their foreflippers, or rubbing their hindflippers together as if trying to scrape off mud. The habit of lying in muddy wallows also helps relieve irritation. If the seals are on the beach they will flick sand over themselves with their flippers. They do this more often in dry weather so it is probably a method of dampening the skin.

While lying in the wallows or on the beach an elephant seal is very loath to move. As one walks around the wallows one's movements are followed by hundreds of pairs of large, round, limpid eyes, but it is possible to walk right up to the seals, and even prod them, without getting any reactions. Only continuous prodding and kicking will rouse an elephant seal. Then, grumbling at the unwarranted intrusion, it will make its way down the beach. At first it backs down the shore, apparently hoping that the source of annoyance will stop so that it can go back to sleep, and only with further disturbance will it turn around and plough into the sea.

The elephant seals' movements are rather different from those of the other true seals we have met, which heave themselves over the ground with a caterpillar-like movement. Elephant seals use their foreflippers as props to hitch their great bulks over the ground. The largest male elephant seals may be twenty feet long and weigh up to five tons, a large proportion of which is blubber, so moving on land is no easy business. Unless they are very hard pressed, the big bulls are likely to flop down after a few yards with a huge sigh, and rest for a while before continuing the exertion.

Although such an epitome of sloth and idleness on land, elephant seals are transformed on entering the sea. Here their vast bulk is supported by the water and the layer of blubber streamlines their bodies. Although no one knows what speeds they can attain, they must be able to move fast in chase of the fish and squid that they feed on.

The blubber also acts as an insulator. A layer of it covers the whole body with the exception of the face and flippers and prevents the body heat being lost to the surrounding water. The efficiency of the blubber was shown by some Australian biologists. They weighed various parts of the bodies of two elephant seals and found that the blubber equalled a third of the total weight. In older seals the proportion would be greater. The biologists then measured the rate at which the blubber conducted heat, and found that it was very low, about the same as asbestos and other materials that are used as insulators. They also calculated that when an elephant seal is at rest the blubber would prevent any body heat being lost to freezing sea water. So elephant seals, and presumably other Antarctic animals with layers of blubber such as other seals, whales and penguins, suffer no strain from living in cold water. When these animals are swimming they will, of course, produce more heat in the body. To prevent themselves from overheating, blood is passed through vessels just under the skin, just as happens to us when our faces have "gone red" through exertion.

Throughout the moulting period the elephant seals fast, but when this is over they start to feed again, and in the winter they disappear from the shores and, until spring, spend all their time out at sea to the north of the pack ice.

The breeding season starts in September, when the big

bulls come ashore. A bull elephant seal is sexually mature when five years old, but it will not start breeding until it is twelve or more. By this time it is a very large animal. Until the females haul out, the bulls pass the time, when they are awake, threatening each other and fighting.

The larger bulls have fairly prominent noses, but it is in the breeding season that they really live up to their name of elephant seals. By muscular action and blood pressure the nose is inflated like a cushion and hangs down over the mouth. The grotesquely enlarged nose and the loud roars and bellows are used to threaten other seals. Presumably they make an elephant seal look very fierce to its rivals. Sometimes threats are not enough and the bulls resort to blows. Coming face to face, they rear up so that over half the body is off the ground. Then, each in turn throws itself against its opponent's breast, sending ripples down the blubber, as if they were two gigantic jellies.

The females start arriving a fortnight or so after the bulls. At first they wander around, then they congregate in groups called harems. Each harem is dominated by one of the big bulls who threatens and fights any other bull who comes too near. There are usually two or three dozen cows to each harem, but there may be as many as a hundred, although in these cases the harem usually becomes split up as it is too large to be defended by one bull.

A week after they come ashore each cow bears a single pup. Unlike its dull grey-brown parents, the pup is covered with a coat of bright black fur. When it is born it has very little blubber and this coat, which all seal pups are born with, helps to keep them warm. However, like the Weddell

*Male elephant seals*

seal pups, the elephant seal pups put on weight very rapidly. Weighing 100 pounds when born, they are four times that when they are weaned at the age of only three weeks. Until then they will never have strayed from their mothers, who keep the other mothers away and also fend off the big bull, for he is quite likely to squash a pup under his vast bulk. Once they are weaned they are abandoned by their mothers and collect together on the borders of the harem where they complete the shedding of their puppy fur. Then they start moving down the beach, searching under stones for small crustaceans and eventually enter the water and start to learn how to find their own food.

Meanwhile, at the harems the point of all the bulls' aggressiveness is becoming clear. For all his bellowing the big bull, called the "harem bull" or "beachmaster," has served no purpose, for the cows will come ashore, congregate and bear their pups even if there are no bulls about, as sometimes happens on some Antarctic islands where there are very few elephant seals. But once the pups are out of the way, mating takes place and we can see that the bull's protection of his harem means that only he is able to mate with the cows. At least, this is the theory; in practice the not-so-big bulls are often able to enter the harem while the beachmaster is occupied on the other side. Even the small bulls are able to mate with the cows as the latter make their way down to the sea. In the end however, it is likely that most of the next year's pups will be the children of the harem bulls, and so be the progeny of what must be the fittest of the elephant seals. For only a few of the males live until they are big enough to hold a harem.

98

After mating, the seals go back to the sea to feed, for they will not have eaten anything since they came ashore to breed. When they have fed they come ashore to moult, and with them come the sealers.

The thick layer of blubber that covers an elephant seal can be boiled down to make a clear oil, on average ninety gallons from each seal. This made it worthwhile for sealers from Europe and America to come down and slaughter the elephant seals. Nothing could be simpler, for the massacre is organized along the lines of a grouse shoot. Beaters armed with poles drive the seals down to the water's edge where marksmen quickly despatch them. The skin and blubber is cut off the carcass and towed out by a dinghy to a waiting ship.

By the beginning of this century elephant seals were becoming very rare because the sealers were killing them indiscriminately. Luckily, when the numbers became so few, it was not worth the sealers' while to go down to the Antarctic, and the elephant seals have been able to recover. On South Georgia the numbers recovered sufficiently for sealing to continue, this time under strict supervision. No pups or cows are killed, and only a fixed number of bulls may be killed in any one season.

# CHAPTER ELEVEN

# Fur Seals

On the islands on either side of the Antarctic Convergence live the fur seals. There are seven species in the southern hemisphere, six of them along the coasts of Australia, South America and South Africa, but only one lives in the cold waters of the sub-Antarctic. This is the Kerguelen fur seal, of which there are two distinct types, or subspecies. One lives to the north of the Convergence, on the islands of Tristan da Cunha, Gough, Marion, Prince Edward, Crozet, Amsterdam and St. Paul, and the other lives to the south, on South Georgia, South Sandwiches, South Orkneys, South Shetlands and Bouvet and Kerguelen.

Fur seals are the only Antarctic representatives of the eared seals. They look very much like the more familiar sea lions of zoos and circuses. Their foreflippers are long and paddlelike and they can tuck their hindflippers under their bodies so that they can lift them up and gallop over the ground far faster than the true seals who can only flop along. The small ears and blunt muzzle, bearing long whiskers, give the fur seals a bear-like appearance, which is reflected in their scientific name of *Arctocephalus* or bearhead.

In habits, the fur seals are very much like the elephant

seals. The females collect in crowds on beaches to have their pups and the older bulls divide the breeding groups into harems which they defend against each other. This is very different from the way the Weddell and other true seals of the Antarctic behave, where the male only comes near the pups by accident and mating seems to be entirely promiscuous.

The fur seal bulls start staking out territories in October and fighting is frequent. The boundaries of the territories are often marked by a rock or some other prominent feature and the fights are concentrated along these boundaries. As each bull knows where his territory ends, the fights rarely come to more than a roaring and slashing match. While the seal is in his territory he will feel brave and aggressive, but as soon as he leaves it he becomes insecure. So the bulls shout and threaten across the boundary, neither daring to come out and fight. The younger bulls either run the gauntlet of the harem bulls and dash up the beach to wait around inland, or stay in the water offshore.

The cows, who are much smaller than the bulls, come ashore in November and collect together on the beach, ignoring the bulls. At this stage the cows are concerned with pupping and the bulls with defending their territory. Any cow that wishes to move along the beach is free to do so.

After the pups have been born the cows take more notice of the bulls, in order to guard their pups from being squashed. If a bull comes too close a cow will snap at his whiskers, making him stop dead in his tracks. (This trait has been put to good use by sealers and other men. On meeting an aggressive bull, they charm him by tickling his whiskers with a stick). Later the pups gather in groups away from the bulls. When their mothers come back from fishing they find their pups by calling. The pups call back until their mothers reach them and identities are confirmed by smell.

It is the habit of herding together in the breeding season that has been the cause of the extinction of some populations of fur seal and the near extinction of others. Nearly every species of seal has been exploited at one time or another for its skin, blubber or meat, but it is only where they herd together on beaches that the sealers have been able to wreak such slaughter. Also fur seals, as their name suggests, have much finer pelts than other seals so that there was a greater inducement to hunt them. Seal fur is made up of groups of hairs. In each group, which sprouts from a single hole in the skin, there is one long stiff guard hair with a number of short, soft hairs behind it. The guard hair prevents the skin being rubbed against rocks, while the short hairs that make up the underfur trap bubbles of air, so providing insulation while the seal is swimming. Fur seal skins are valuable because they have more short hairs to each group than other seals, and these provide a soft, thick fur, when the guard hairs have been removed.

Captain Cook found large herds of fur seals when he discovered South Georgia on his voyage around the Southern Ocean. He reported his findings at home and within a few years sealing ships were on their way south. The crews lived a very hard life, their ships being small even by the standards of those days. On reaching the breeding beaches, parties were put ashore to kill and skin the seals. While ashore they lived in crude shelters whose remains are still to be seen today. They were usually no more than low walls of boulders in the shelter of cliffs and would have been roofed with seal skins. Here many of the sealers died, being marooned or drowned after their small ships were wrecked. But the rewards of a successful sealing trip were immense and, despite the hardships, there was no shortage of men willing to risk their lives.

Killing the seals was a simple matter, for, like the elephant seals, the fur seals are largely unafraid of Man, especially when they have pups. Once the harem bulls had been despatched, the sealers could walk through the harems clubbing the cows and pups. Around the year 1800, there were thirty sealing ships visiting South Georgia alone, and one vessel alone took about 50,000 skins. As many of these were from cows and pups it is not surprising that numbers dropped and by 1822 the sealers had turned to the less lucrative elephant seals, having taken a million and a half fur seal skins since 1800.

Fifty years later the numbers had risen sufficiently for another onslaught to be launched, after which it was thought that they must have become extinct. Many years later a colony was found on Bird Island, near South Georgia, and in 1949 a few cows and pups were found both in the South Shetlands, which had been one of the strongholds of southern fur seals, and in the South Orkneys. There are now thought to be over 20,000 on South Georgia and the small colonies elsewhere seem to be

*Fur seals*

expanding, so that it has even been suggested that the Antarctic fur seals will provide furs again, as the northern fur seals of Alaska are already doing under strict supervision.

# CHAPTER TWELVE

# The Giant Whales

Giant whales are the largest animals that have ever lived. The biggest found was 100 feet long and weighed 130 tons. This is four times the weight of the giant, extinct dinosaurs, and is equal to 30 elephants or 1,600 men. Whales have only been able to grow so large because they have taken to living in the sea, where their bodies are supported by the water. They just would not have been able to survive on legs, and it is very likely that the big dinosaurs spent most of their lives in rivers and swamps so that the strain on their legs would have been reduced by the buoyancy of their bodies.

There are about fifty species of Cetacea, the group of mammals to which the whales, porpoises and dolphins belong. It is divided into two principal groups, the Mysticeti or whalebone whales and the Odontoceti or toothed whales. Many of these species are to be found in the Southern Ocean but we will only be concerned here with some of them. Among the whalebone whales there are the rorqual whales including the blue whale, sei whale, fin whale and humpback whale. These four provide most of the catches of the whaling fleets, and the blue and humpback whales may be on the verge of extinction. The two important toothed whales are the sperm whale and the killer whale, which is really a dolphin.

How the whales developed into aquatic animals is not known for certain because very few fossil whales have been found, and these were already adapted for life in the seas so that they would have been unable to come out on land. It seems very possible that the whales originated from the same ancestors as the hoofed mammals like sheep and cattle, but since then have undergone enormous bodily changes.

In Chapter 9 some of the adaptations of seals to an aquatic way of life were discussed. Whales face the same problems but to a greater degree, for they are wholly committed to the sea. Seals come out on land, or onto the pack ice, to breed and to rest, but whales must stay in the water. Their bodies are modified to such an extent that if a whale does come ashore, it is stranded and will inevitably die. To discuss the modifications in detail would take longer than space will allow and even then the picture would be far from complete because there are still large gaps in our knowledge.

Merely looking at a picture of a whale, or its skeleton, will show the whales' fitness for an aquatic life. Seals have hind limbs, attached to a pelvis in the normal way, but these are absent in whales. All that is left is a small bone, a remnant of the pelvis. Consequently, whales swim in the same way as fish, by rhythmically thrashing their tails. The difference is that whales move their tail up and down, instead of from side to side, and their flukes, as the fins are called, are set horizontally instead of vertically, as in a fish. In the course of becoming a swimming organ the structure of the tail has been modified. There are many more vertebrae in the tails of whales than in other mammals and they are flat, rather like draught counters. This gives the tail greater flexibility. Running along the top of the backbone is a crest made up of flat spines, or processes, projecting from each vertebra. This is the anchor for the powerful swimming muscles.

The forelimbs are still present, but have been changed in shape to form flippers for use in steering. The bones of the flippers show how the whales are related to other mammals, as they have five fingers just as we have. However, the five fingers in a whale's flipper are rather different from ours. The two middle fingers have many more bones, from ten to fourteen instead of three. These two much elongated fingers give the whale's hand its flipper shape.

The first signs of whales that an observer sees from a ship are puffs of fine spray. Each time a whale surfaces, it expels air from its lungs and this forms a cloud of spray, known as the blow or *blåst* by the whalers. At one time sailors thought that the blow was a jet of water, like a geyser, and this is how it is shown in old pictures. Nowadays it is thought that it is produced in roughly the same way as our "steaming breath" on a cold day. As warm air from the lungs meets the cold air outside, it condenses to form a cloud. This is not the whole story because whale blows can also be seen in the tropics. The explanation here is that while in the whales' lungs the air is under pressure but as it is expelled the pressure is suddenly released. When any such matter is put under pressure and then released, its temperature drops, so this is why the whales' breath condenses.

If the observer on the ship is very lucky a whale may blow only a few yards away and he will see its blowhole open and shut. The blowhole is the whale's nostril, which is surrounded by a thick band of elastic tissue and muscle to make it very watertight. The top of the head seems to be the obvious place for a whale to have its blowhole as it will be able to breathe without raising its head out of the water. Yet when we remember that whales are probably descended from cattlelike animals, it is difficult to see how the nostrils came to be at the top of the head instead of at the tip of the snout. To understand the positioning of the blowhole we must understand the structure of the whale's head. The skull has been pulled out to form a long beak so that the brain is set right at the back of the head and the bones of the forehead have become compressed. The nostrils therefore appear to have moved up to the top of the head. When you realize how the skull has changed, you can see why the whale's head looks so grotesque.

Each time it blows, a whale breathes out and in once, so it is easy to count the number of times that it breathes in a minute. The figure is surprisingly low, once or twice per minute, as compared to fifteen or sixteen for a man. Furthermore, a whale's lungs are smaller, compared to the size of its body, than a man's. We would expect faster breathing and larger lungs as the whale needs to be able to quickly replace the oxygen used by its body in a long dive. In fact, it is able to do so by efficiently changing the air in the lungs. When we breathe in and out only one eighth of the air in the lungs is changed, but a whale is able to change seven-eighths. We take four seconds to breathe in and out, and only one litre of air passes through our nostrils, but a rorqual whale displaces about 1,500 litres in less than two seconds.

The rapid changing of air means that whales need spend very little time at the surface, although after a deep dive they will spend some time at the surface, breathing fairly rapidly. They have the same sort of adaptations for diving as the seals. Their pulse rate drops and blood is circulated only to essential organs such as brain, heart and muscles. One difference is that whales breathe in before submerging, whereas seals breathe out.

It has long been known that sperm whales dive to great depths as their bodies have been found entangled in submarine cables brought up for repairs. More recently, it has been shown that whalebone whales can dive to great depths, as is shown by experiments in which special harpoons with depth gauges attached were fired at rorqual whales. When the whales were secured they were found to have dived to depths of over 1,000 feet. Obviously these dives were something of an emergency procedure and it is unlikely that they normally go very deep, for the krill and squid on which the whales feed live near the surface.

It seems odd that the largest animals that ever lived should eat nothing but small crustaceans, yet the crustaceans that live in the surface layers of the sea are one of the few forms of life that exist in sufficient quantities to provide food for the great whales. In the Southern Ocean the abundance of whales is due to the vast masses of krill and other crustaceans which make the ocean richer than any other part of the world.

The rorqual whales have a special device for collecting krill in large numbers. Instead of teeth they have two sets of whalebone plates, or baleen hanging from the roof of the mouth. Each plate is triangular, broad at the top and tapering to a point below and about half an inch from its neighbours. The scientific name of the baleen whales, Mysticeti, is derived from the Greek *mystax* meaning moustache. This is because the inner edge of each plate is frayed and looks like a sort of internal moustache. The baleen is made up of modified hair, in the same way as rhinoceros horn is made of compressed hair. The shreds formed by the fraying are interwoven to form a dense mat on which the krill are caught.

When it finds a dense shoal of krill the whale opens its mouth and sucks them in. Then the mouth is shut and the tongue is pushed up to the roof of the mouth, squeezing the water out through the baleen. The krill are caught in the meshes of the baleen and swallowed. The same method of feeding is used by the crabeater seals. Filter feeding, as it is called, is used by many animals that live on plankton. Herring live on small planktonic animals, but they do not gulp in mouthfuls of food and squirt water out of their mouths. Instead they swim along with their mouths open with the water streaming out through their gill openings, and their food is caught on special filters on the gills. Krill are also filter feeders, collecting minute plants on comb-like projections on their legs and passing them to their mouths.

During the Antarctic summer the great rorqual whales gather in areas where there is a vast harvest to be reaped. Sometimes their diet includes a few extras, for fish and penguins have been found in their stomachs. Presumably these animals were also feeding on the krill and were accidentally sucked in. How the swarms of krill are found is rather a mystery. It is known that whales use a system of echo-location similar to the asdic or sonar used by the navy for hunting submarines, but even with our advanced electronics we have not been able to make an echo-location system sensitive enough to detect krill. However they do it, the whales are able to collect enough food to build up thick deposits of blubber. In some species the body is covered by a layer a foot thick.

In the autumn the whales move northward. The Antarctic seas are beginning to freeze over so that the whales cannot surface to blow and there are fewer krill to eat. Because there is less to eat the whales move to warmer water where they will not have to use up so much energy to keep warm. They also breed in warmer waters. This is necessary because the single calf that each female bears every other year is born with very little blubber, so it would have difficulty keeping itself warm in cold seas.

The mother whale takes great care of her offspring. As soon as it is born she assists it to the surface so that it can take its first breath. Once it has filled its lungs it is buoyant enough to come to the surface by itself. The calf's baleen does not grow until it is six months old. Until then it lives on its mother's milk. It takes a teat in the side of its mouth, but instead of the calf sucking, milk is pumped into it by contraction of muscles around the mother's milk gland. A large volume of milk is transferred from mother to calf in a few seconds, as the calf is unable to stay submerged for long and has to surface between sucks. Even when it is able to feed itself the calf stays with its mother, not leaving her until it is nearly a year old.

Apart from the baleen whales and the squid-eating sperm whales, there is another kind of whale in Antarctic waters. This is the killer whale, well-named, for it preys on other animals. It even attacks the big blue whales, falling on them in packs of up to forty. They tear at the blue whales' flippers, lips and tongues, then leave them to die from loss of blood before devouring them. An example of their voracity is shown by a killer whale, which, when captured, had the remains of thirteen porpoises and fourteen seals in its stomach. Nothing is safe from killer whales. They are to be found all over the world and in some places they cause great damage to fisheries. Luckily, they are rarely dangerous to Man because they stay in deep water, away from beaches. However, there are stories of Antarctic explorers out on ice floes when killer whales have tried to spill the men and their dogs into the water by tipping the floes up with their snouts.

*Killer whales*

# CHAPTER THIRTEEN

# The Sad Story of Whaling

No account of whales would be complete without a description of whaling. If it had not been for whaling, whales would not be on the verge of extinction today, but it is through whaling that we have learnt something of their habits. The earliest record we have of whales is from the Stone Age, when a primitive man scratched the outline of a whale on a piece of rock at Røddøy in Norway. This drawing is believed to have been made nearly 4,000 years ago. It seems likely that from earliest times men have made use of the carcasses of stranded whales, but less certain is the extent to which whales were actively hunted. Early records show that the Vikings and the Japanese hunted whales in small boats, harpooning them or chasing them up fjords so that they became stranded.

These hunts were run on a part-time basis. Watchers on the shore would alert the boatmen, who dropped what they were doing and set out after the whales. The first professional whaling was carried out by the Basques in the Bay of Biscay. As they killed off the whales around the coasts of Europe they had to hunt farther afield, crossing the Atlantic to Newfoundland. Later they were joined by the British and Dutch and spread into Arctic seas. The whales they hunted were called right whales, merely because they were the right kind of whales to hunt. Their cruising speed was 2 knots with a maximum of 5 knots in emergency, so it was possible to chase them in rowing boats. Also, they were easy to handle, as the corpses floated.

In the eighteenth and nineteenth centuries the sperm whale was also hunted. This was the Golden Age of whaling, immortalized by Herman Melville's *Moby Dick*, when ships quartered the oceans in search of whales and came home with immensely rich cargoes of oil. By the middle of the nineteenth century several species of the right whales were nearly extinct and the sperm whale was rare. The final decline of this industry set in when mineral oil came to replace whale oil in lamps and candles.

Then, in 1868, came a revolutionary invention. Svend Føyn, a Norwegian, invented a harpoon gun which could be mounted in the bows of a steamship. Now the fast rorqual or fin whales could be chased and caught, and the scene was set for the onslaught on the last stronghold of the great whales. Another Norwegian, C.A. Larsen, had been to the Antarctic and had seen large numbers of whales around South Georgia and the small islands off the tip of the Antarctic Peninsula. In 1904 he set up a whaling factory at Grytviken, at the top of a fjord in South Georgia. Within a few years factories had sprung up all around this part of the Antarctic and factory ships were cruising around the open waters.

The factory ships were an important development in whaling. Instead of the whale carcass having to be towed some distance to the factory on the shore, they need only be taken to the factory ship which steams around the ocean. Factory ships are equipped with a slipway in the stern so that the carcasses can be hauled onto the main deck and cut up.

Each factory ship is accompanied by 7 to 18 whale catchers. These are trawler-sized ships specially constructed for chasing and harpooning the whales. As soon as the look-out in the crow's-nest sights a whale, the chase is on. Aided by powerful engines the catcher bears down on the whale, which dives to safety. Eventually it has to come to the surface to breathe, only to find that the catcher is still after it, and so it dives again. Soon the whale is worn down and the catcher can get within harpoon range. The captain runs down the special gangway from the bridge to the high bows where the harpoon gun is ready loaded. By hand signals he gives orders to the helmsman to steer the catcher right up to the whale. This is not an easy business. Visibility is often bad and the waves buffet the ship which leaps around, rolling and twisting. Even more difficult is sighting the gun, but whaling captains rely on their skill for their jobs. Each man in the whaling fleet is paid on a bonus system and the more whales a captain shoots, the more money his crew gets. So the captain stands behind his gun, exposed to the spray breaking over the bows, and, as the whale appears beneath him, he pulls the trigger. The heavy iron harpoon smashes into the whale's body and the grenade in its head explodes, mortally wounding the animal. The whale's immediate reaction is to dive, dragging hundreds of feet of harpoon cable after it.

Any fisherman would know that even with the stoutest

rope it would be foolish to try and pull the whale straight in. It must be played gently to prevent the rope being snapped. Accordingly, the captain stays in the bows and gives orders to the ship's engineer to control the winch, taking in slack as the whale surfaces or paying it out if it dives. There is still a danger of the rope being snapped, for there will be a terrific strain on it as the catcher bounces over the waves, or if the whale suddenly changes direction. A fisherman reduces sudden strains on his line with the flexible rod, but no rod could be built to cope with an eighty-ton whale. Instead a spring system is used to reduce the sudden jerks on the line. The line passes through a pulley on the mast and down to the winch. This pulley is attached to a cable that runs up to the masthead, over another pulley and down to a large spring at the base of the mast. If the ship suddenly lurches, tightening the line, the pulley hanging from the mast is pulled down and the spring is stretched up, easing the tension.

When the wounded whale is tired out, it is brought alongside and killed with another harpoon. The carcass has then to be pumped up with compressed air because rorquals sink when they are dead. Finally the body is set free to be collected later and towed to the factory ship.

Life on a whale catcher is not comfortable as it plunges through the seas in one of the stormiest parts of the world. With its large engines, it is not built for comfort, but neither is the much larger factory ship, even though some of them have been converted from passenger liners. The factory ships have to process the whales before they decompose, so the men must work long shifts, in all weathers.

_Gunner on a whaling ship about to fire at a whale_

A whaling factory in action is a slaughterhouse run on the lines of an iron foundry, with the stench of whale blubber pervading every corner and a pall of smoke and steam hanging over it. The whale carcasses are drawn up the stern slipway and onto the plan, a large wooden-floored "courtyard", where they are immediately attacked by the flensers. With razor-sharp, long-handled knives, known as flensing knives, they cut grooves in the blubber from tail flukes to head. Wires are attached to the blubber, steam winches rattle and the strips of blubber are pulled off like a banana skin. Now the blubber cutters run forward, pull the strips away, cut them into squares and feed them into the boilers—huge revolving pressure cookers which render the blubber down to a clear oil.

Meanwhile the carcass is being pulled farther along the plan while another is drawn up from the sea. The lemmers come forward now and start cutting the meat from the bones. Great chunks are carried off on conveyor belts either to be boiled up for the oil they contain, or to be frozen and carried home in refrigerator ships for consumption by humans or their pets. By now the plan is covered with blood and blubber, making movements hazardous. The plan workers wear spikes in their boots to give them a grip on the greasy surface. Even so, the wires from winches, pieces of gut or blubber and the rolling of the factory ship conspire to send an unwary man flying, perhaps into the open mouth of a blubber boiler.

Whaling was a hazardous occupation in the days of Moby Dick, and it has not changed over the years. Every land-based whaling station in the Antarctic Islands has its cemetery where crosses commemorate men lost in accidents on the plan or at sea. Some record the loss of a whale catcher that foundered with all hands in a storm. Despite this miserable life men are still found to run the factories and despite the decline in the numbers of whales it is still worthwhile to send ships down to the Antarctic to chase them.

What is it that makes it so worthwhile? Since earliest times the discovery of a stranded whale has meant a time of plenty to its finders. One whale provided many tons of meat which would feed many mouths for many days. As man became more sophisticated, he found more uses for the carcass. The blubber could be melted down to oil for use in lighting, cooking or lubrication. The whalebone could be used for a variety of things in an age which did not know spring steel or plastics. Parts for machinery, corsets, peaks of uniform caps, and fishing rods were all made out of whalebone.

The value of a whale carcass is shown by the figures for 17th-century whaling expeditions. The ships cost about £1,200 to fit out. This was a lot of money in those days, but the profits, providing the ship was not wrecked, were enormous. Each whale caught would give 25 tons of oil and perhaps 1½ tons of whalebone, and whalebone was worth over £2,000 a ton. So the capture of one whale meant a profit. Nearer our own day the factory ship *Southern Harvester* could process forty whales a day, producing 600 tons of oil and 130 tons of meat, to the value of £50,000. Whale oil is no longer used for lighting and very little for lubrication, but it is now used for food.

Chemists discovered how to turn oil into a solid grease so that nowadays margarine, and soap, are made out of whale oil.

With such profits to be made it is not surprising that the Antarctic whales should have suffered in consequence. Their last stronghold has been breached and it is feared that some species, such as the giant blue whale, may become extinct. It is also not surprising that someone should have felt the need to try to conserve the whales, and in 1920 the Discovery Committee was formed by the British Colonial Office. The aim of the Committee was to investigate the seas around South Georgia, for it was essential that we should have a knowledge of the whale's way of life if the whales were to be saved.

In Chapter 2 we saw how the R.R.S. *Discovery*, commissioned by the Discovery Committee, ranged over the Southern Ocean gathering data on the temperature of the sea, the numbers of plankton and other subjects. These were then related to the numbers of whales caught in different places. Whales were found to be most common where the krill was concentrated, which is not surprising as the large rorqual whales feed mainly on krill. Also, the concentrations of krill were related to the concentration of various chemicals in the sea. Here was a method of forecasting where the most whales were to be found and nowadays whaling fleets carry scientists who analyze sea water, collect the plankton and advise the whalers on how to plan their voyage.

Meanwhile, at the whaling stations on South Georgia, other biologists from the *Discovery* were examining the whale carcasses as they were brought in. This was not an easy job, for the flensers and lemmers were not going to stop working and lose money, so the scientists had to run around the whale, avoiding wires and lumps of slippery blubber, to measure its length and cut out various organs. They collected samples of food from its stomach, noted its sex, looked to see if it was pregnant or whether there was any milk to show if it had had a baby with it. Armed with this information the biologists were able to work out how long a female whale carried her baby before it was born, how long it stayed with her, when it started to breed itself and how rapidly it grew.

The aim of this research was to find out how many whales could be killed each year without their becoming extinct. One thing was obvious, at the rate of killing after World War I, the Antarctic whales would soon cease to exist. So, after several attempts, an International Whaling Commission was set up in which representatives of nations engaged in Antarctic whaling would work out, with the assistance of the biologists, how many whales could be killed each year. The total was divided up between each nation and each was allowed to kill only its own quota. The quota system was based on B.W.U. or the "Blue Whale Unit." One blue whale equalled 1 B.W.U. as did two fin whales and six sei whales, so a nation with a quota of 2,000 B.W.U. could catch 2,000 blue whales, 4,000 fin whales, 12,000 sei whales or any combination of these. The Whaling Commission also sought to stop the killing of females with young and immature whales.

Unfortunately, the theory of the International Whaling

Commission has not always been borne out in practice. The whaling companies would not restrict their hunting as much as the scientists would have liked, because to do so would have meant a loss of money. Yet the annual catch has gone down from 42,000 whales in 1930 to 22,000 in 1963. This is not due to caution on the part of the whalers but due to the rarity of the whales. The fin whale population dropped from 110,000 in 1955 to 33,000 in 1963 and it was estimated that there were only 1,000 blue whales left. Being such slow-breeding animals they may never regain their numbers.

That this should happen is sheer stupidity, or greed, on the part of the whalers, for the biologists have told them that if they will only limit their catch they will be able to make a worthwhile profit year after year without reducing the total number of whales. In other words, the whales will be able to breed as fast as they are hunted.

What hope is there? In 1967 the Commission agreed to refrain from killing all blue whales and humpbacks and that some areas of the Southern Ocean were to be reserves where no hunting could take place. This co-operation by the whaling nations in welcome news, but what about the gunner who sees every whale as an addition to his bonus?

# CHAPTER FOURTEEN

# Insects and Others

All the animals we have met in previous chapters have been intimately connected with the sea. They have spent most, if not all, their lives either swimming in or flying over the sea in search of food. The whales, fish, crustaceans and others are completely at home in the water. The birds and seals spend most of their time in water although they must return to land to breed. There are a few possible exceptions: skuas may obtain most of their food by preying on other birds during the breeding season, but they have to go to sea in the winter, and sheathbills, although land birds, obtain much of their food from the shore. It would seem, then, that the land mass of Antarctica is of little importance to biologists. But a closer scrutiny of the snow-free areas, around the fringes of the bird colonies and in places where mosses and lichens grow, reveals that there are some true land animals, even if very small. About twenty species have been found, mainly small insects and mites, and more are being discovered every year. Such creatures generally go unnoticed, and if noticed they fail to arouse interest or amusement as do the more spectacular animals. They are, nevertheless, important in that the continent of Antarctica is, in places, far from incapable of supporting life as it appears at first sight to be.

*Animals of the Antarctic*

It is true that the vast bulk of the continent is covered with ice, and so is lifeless, but in a small part of it, perhaps 3,000 square miles out of a total of five and a half million, conditions are suitable for life, at least during the summer. This includes small patches around the coasts, especially along the Antarctic peninsula and in valleys by the Ross Sea, where there are bare rocks sparsely covered by lichens, algae and mosses. Only in these places is there water and a minimum of warmth, sufficient to maintain life. It is because these two things are lacking over most of the continent that so few kinds of creatures are able to live in Antarctica.

It is difficult to appreciate that Antarctica is a desert because we normally think of deserts as being hot, sandy areas. But there can be cold deserts, for a desert is simply a place with very low rainfall. Antarctica is covered with water, but in the form of ice which is no use to animals. There are also heavy and frequent snowstorms but much of the snow in the air is merely being blown from one place to another, and, anyway, if snow is melted down it makes very little water. So Antarctic land animals, like those living in the hot sands of the Sahara Desert, must be able to resist drying up, or find a place where water is in constant supply if only in small quantities.

Water can be found in Antarctica where the ground is warm enough to melt the ice and snow. In the Antarctic peninsula, for example, the air is warm enough in midsummer to melt the snow, but there are other places where, even though the air temperature is well below freezing point, the snow still melts because of the strength

128

of the sun's rays. Even a short distance from the South Pole the heating effect of the sun can be quite striking. In three hours a rock surface can, at certain times, rise seventy-five degrees from a numbing twenty-five degrees of frost to a comfortably warm temperature. In summer, enough snow and ice may melt to form streams which run down the hills and fill ponds and lakes in the valleys.

The plants, mosses, lichens, algae and, in the Antarctic peninsula, a few grasses, grow in these wet places, and in the vegetation live the small animals. Where conditions are suitable these animals can be found in surprisingly large numbers. A stone may be covered with a mass of what appear to be minute black beetles, but are in fact mites, eight-legged relatives of spiders very much like the more familiar harvest-bugs. The mites feed either on algae or on fungi that grow on the dead and decaying plants.

Fungi, plants and the corpses of other small animals form the diet of the other invertebrate, or backboneless creatures. These include a few kinds of springtails, primitive wingless insects found elsewhere all over the world. Sometimes they can be found actually on the snow on Antarctica, and in such large numbers as to make the snow look less white. Another insect found in Antarctica is an unusual fly. A mere 3/16 of an inch long, it is in fact the largest Antarctic land animal and is related to the midges that are such a plague on summer evenings in temperate regions. But the strange feature of the Antarctic fly is that it has no wings. The springtails also do not have wings, but their ancestors never had any either. They appeared in the world before insects had developed the power of flight. On the other hand the Antarctic fly's ancestors were able to fly, as do its relatives the midges.

To be wingless is no disadvantage for an Antarctic insect. The air is far too cold for insects to fly; their muscles just would not work well enough. Birds are able to do so because they are warm-blooded so their muscles are kept warm and birds can be active even when it is very cold.

Apart from the mites, springtails and the fly which are all arthropods, the great group of animals with hard bodies and jointed legs, there are some worms, such as round-worms, living in the moss and feeding on the plants.

For all these small animals life is difficult. Their surroundings freeze up for eight or nine months of the year and even in summer they are liable to be frozen up at any moment, especially at night or if the sky is clouded. The snow affords them some protection, acting as an insulator, for even though the air temperature can drop tens of degrees below zero, the temperature under two or three feet of snow stays within a few degrees of freezing point. At this temperature they can still move around, but their water supply will have frozen up. Under these circumstances they protect themselves by shutting up shop, as it were. The roundworms and some of the arthropods merely dry up and remain in a state of suspended animation until there is a thaw. Others are unable to do this and the adults die but the species survive because the eggs they have laid can survive the hard weather to hatch later.

A less hazardous life is led by the small animals that live

*A summer scene in the Antarctic*

in the freshwater pools. Once the ice has melted, the pools stay open until the autumn. During this short season algae grow rapidly, providing food for small crustaceans, the freshwater counterparts of the marine krill and amphipods. No more than a quarter of an inch long, the freshwater shrimps swim around the mats of algae that cover the stones on the bottom or float near the surface. They scrape up particles of algae with their comblike legs, and push them into their mouths. Like the mites and springtails the freshwater animals can sometimes be found in numbers so vast that the water seems to be choked with them. Unless the pools are very shallow, they do not freeze solid in the winter and a few of the crustaceans in them survive and continue breeding. When the pool does freeze solid only the eggs survive the winter.

One reason, perhaps, why freshwater shrimps are so common in the Antarctic is that their natural enemies in other parts of the world, the fishes, are absent. On the other hand, they do have some enemies. One of the large species of freshwater shrimp has hooked rather than comblike legs with which it grapples other shrimps and tears them apart. Antarctic terns sometimes fly over pools, dipping down to catch freshwater shrimps.

How these small animals, both land-living and freshwater, got to Antarctica is a question that has long interested the zoologists. We saw in Chapter I that at one time Antarctica was connected to other continents and had a tropical climate. But for a long time it was covered with ice and it has been estimated that only in the last 10,000 years has the ice receded sufficiently to leave the small snow-free areas and the pools. It seems most likely that the minute animals could have been brought from the continents of Africa, South America or Australia either on the feet of birds or borne by the wind. Experiments have shown that minute creatures can be carried by wind. Fine meshed nets erected on long poles or on aeroplanes have collected a wide variety of small organisms in the air over Antarctica. Birds may also bring over animals or their eggs in mud on their feet or feathers, but this is less likely because the birds that nest in the Antarctic do not usually visit other lands and, anyway, such animals would probably be killed or washed off when the birds land on the sea.

Whatever may have been the means of transport that brought the mites, springtails and the other small animals to Antarctica, there is no doubt about how another class of small animals gets there. These are the parasites living on the larger animals, eating their flesh or blood or taking their food, sometimes killing them in the process. Skuas and dominican gulls that steal fish from shags are sometimes called parasites but in the strict sense the name should be applied to fleas and lice that live on the skin or tapeworms living in the intestine. The animal unwillingly providing them with food is called, almost ironically, the host.

Many seals and birds in the Antarctic are hosts to parasites. Penguins may be infested with biting lice that crawl around in their feathers eating fragments of dead skin or feathers. They have hooks on their legs and can run very quickly, as indeed they must if they are to avoid being killed when the bird preens itself. Another kind of parasite, the sucking louse, is found on seals. They burrow into their hosts' skin and suck their blood.

The greatest problem for the parasites is survival when the host enters the water. They are then in danger of drowning or freezing. Drowning is avoided because air is trapped in the host's fur or feathers as it dives. On the other hand the skin temperature of the host drops below freezing when it is in the water. As seals and penguins spend most of their lives at sea this makes survival difficult for the lice. They can overcome this by going into a state of suspended animation; they feed only occasionally and their body processes work very slowly. Seal lice are most numerous on the flippers where the lack of blubber allows the body heat to escape, which means that the flippers are warmer than the rest of the body.

The sucking louse that lives on the elephant seal has to breed during the three months when its host is on land, itself breeding and also moulting. Again, the high temperature in the flippers helps the lice to breed rapidly. They are able to spread easily from one seal to another because of the elephant seals' habit of lying close together while moulting.

The animals discussed in this chapter are small and insignificant. Their names mean nothing except to a specialist. But they have been worth including if only to show that an ice-covered continent, like a sandy desert, is not as completely barren as its general character might suggest. A desert may be too hot or too cold from the point of view of a large animal like Man, but to a small animal less than a quarter of an inch long there are many nooks and crannies providing a suitable climate. This is called the micro-climate and often bears no resemblance to the overall climatic conditions we call the weather. Under a stone or buried in a seal flipper, a small animal can find shelter from the most adverse conditions. It has, in fact, escaped to another world with its own special climate, the micro-climate. The conclusion to be drawn from this is the same as that demonstrated by the strange habits of the emperor penguin. Conditions in the Antarctic, too harsh for humans brought up in temperate climates, are tolerable for animals who have adopted a way of life that enables them to escape the worst extremes of climate.

# Scientific Names

| Leopard seal | *Hydrurga leptonyx* |
| Crabeater seal | *Lobodon carcinophagus* |
| Ross seal | *Ommatophoca rossi* |
| Elephant seal | *Mirounga leonina* |
| Fur seal | *Arctocephalus australis* |
| Blue whale | *Sibbaldus musculus* |
| Fin whale | *Balaenoptera physalus* |
| Sei whale | *B. acutorostrata* |
| Humpback whale | *Megaptera novaeangliae* |
| Right whale | *Eubalaena* |
| Sperm whale | *Physeter catodon* |
| Killer whale | *Orcinus orca* |

*Fish*

| Antarctic cod | *Nototheniidae* |
| Bloodless or crocodile fish | *Chaenichthyidae* |

*Some Invertebrates*

| Krill | *Euphausia superba* |
| Amphipods | *Amphipoda* |
| Whale louse | *Cyamus* |
| Wingless fly | *Belgica antarctica* |
| Mites | *Acarina* |
| Springtails | *Collembola* |
| Limpet | *Patinigra antarctica* |
| Sea gooseberries and comb jellies | *Ctenophora* |

# Bibliography

Backhouse, K.M. *Seals,* Arthur Barker, 1969.

Carrick, R., Holdgate, M.W. & Prévost, J. ed. *Biologie Antarctique,* Herman, Paris, 1963. (Mostly in English).

Hardy, Sir Alister. *Great Waters,* Collins, 1967.

King, Judith E. *Seals of the World,* British Museum (Natural History), 1964.

Ommanney, F.D. *South Latitude,* Longmans, 1965.

Priestley, Sir Raymond; Adie, R.J.; Robin, G de Q., ed. *Antarctic Research,* Butterworth, 1969.

*Scientific American.* Vol. 207. No. 3. September, 1962. Issue devoted to the Antarctic.

Stonehouse, Bernard. *Penguins,* Arthur Barker, 1969.

# Index

*Printed in Great Britain
by T. & A. Constable Ltd.*

A0000401470497

**BERTRAM WOODS BRANCH**

70-12297 W

70-12297 W

Burton, R.

J

J591.999
B97

Animals of the Antarctic.

4.00

11 '80-1 81-1 83 84-1
85-1

**Shaker Heights Public Library**
3450 Lee Road
Shaker Heights, Ohio

DEMCO

14 DAYS - NOT RENEWABLE